get rad.

"We Cancel Thanksgiving Dinner After the 2016 Election Results" first appeared in *Former People: A Journal of Bangs and Wimpers.* "Walter, Wrongly Convicted" first appeared with the audio art journal *Rocky Mountain Revival.*

ISBN-10: 0-9979499-1-0
ISBN-13: 978-0-9979499-1-9

So Say We All (SSWA) is a San Diego-based 501c3 non-profit organization that provides arts education to populations without access, and supports local artists through showcase opportunities and peer-to-peer counseling.

www.sosayweallonline.com

THE RADVOCATE

VOL II, NO 15

Matt E. Lewis
FOUNDING EDITOR

Julia Dixon Evans
EDITOR

Marco Cerda
EDITORIAL INTERN

Anthony Martin
Ryan Bradford
EDITORIAL ADVISORS

Leesa Cross-Smith
2017 LITERARY PRIZE IN FICTION JUDGE

Keith McCleary
GRAPHIC DESIGNER

Matthew Revert
COVER ARTIST

Justin Hudnall
EXECUTIVE DIRECTOR

Editor's Note

More so now than ever before, vision is a premium. While the amount of new thoughts and ideas haven't diminished, investments in them have—the recession taught us that tightening the belt was not an option, but a way of life we'd have to get used to. While institutions scramble to justify the bare minimum of what they need, creative ventures are often the first things on the chopping block, the kind of thing only a privileged few can afford to have. Whether it's technological enterprise or artistic expression, an investment into something unknown isn't seen as an investment. Over and over again, the safe bet is made, the re-hashing of the tried and true, the option of making a little back preferable to making nothing at all. Risk is a four-letter word—supported by a culture that worships a false mythos that those who try and fail deserve their fate, that stability is only an option for those that have already proven themselves on the killing field of public opinion. Even those who do believe are forced to turn away, unable to sacrifice the time or energy sucked away by the daily grind.

In its infancy, *The Radvocate* was certainly no investment—it was a joke incarnate, a kind of send-off of the marketing of sub-cultures, barely worth the paper it was printed on. In time, support allowed it to grow into something else, a platform for writers and artists desperate to connect and share their work. A network of a few friends grew, first around the country and then around the world. *The Radvocate* resonated with them because it was something different, something more chaotic, something that didn't require constant engagement or pushes to meet marketing numbers. The internet may have been a boon to sharing creative work, but it also made it twice as easy to commoditize it. *The Radvocate* just wanted to fuck up your brain for a little while, to cut through the fuzziness with the shrill voices of other people screaming, "Me too, man. Me too."

Today, *The Radvocate* has grown and matured into the best incarnation of its former self. With the help of the non-profit So Say We All, *The Radvocate* is still alive, paperback-bound, and presenting creative work without advertising or compromise. This latest issue is filled with the kind of expression we believe in, a bold vision in a field where it is so difficult to stand out from the crowd. As the founder, I can think of no better time to step away from *The Radvocate* and pass on the duties to the phenomenal editor, writer, and person, Julia Dixon Evans. Far from being disinterested or tired of creating *The Radvocate*, I rather feel it is the most responsible option to allow a thing to grow when it is strong enough to stand on its own. I know that under Julia's editorship, *The Radvocate* will continue to change and evolve beyond what I could ever hope to accomplish. To have a project survive beyond my involvement is something I am extremely proud of, and I can't wait to read along with you all as Julia and her team help usher us in to the ever-changing future. What you hold in your hands now is a result of the support of you, the reader, and people like you who believe in things that shouldn't work, but do. I dedicate this issue to you, and all those that would fly in the face of convention, one goofy Xerox at a time.

Stay rad,
Matt E. Lewis

CONTENTS

MARISA CRANE
That's Why They Have Coats On   9

AMANDA TUMMINARO
No Smoking   19
The Stewardess   20
Pap Smear   21

PHILIP KUAN
The Request   22

CL BLEDSOE
Swatches   26
Telling the White Man a Secret   28
With the Old Magazines and Spiders   30
The Bean King   31

NICOLE MARTINEZ
Worlds Apart   32

KEVIN MCCOY
ocean – kyle of tongue   38

CAT DIXON
Women in the Workplace   39

BRETT MORRIS
I Wanted To Be A Hero   40

KATHLEEN LANGSTROTH
Primary Education   44

TONI MARTIN
Fool's Gold   49

DAVID HENSON / *illustrated by* LAURA GWYNNE
The Tinder Men   58

LINDA M. CRATE
my hopes and fears   66

DONNA ZEPHRINE
Homeward Bound 67

ELAINE GINGERY
Six Months, Max 68

STEVE TAGUE
The Farm 72

NOLAN HUTTON
Fish hooks hung 80
Single mother trying to use the bathroom 81
Last 4th of July 82

GERARDO DE JESUS GURROLA JR.
Gibbous 83

PAUL DOUGLAS MCNEILL II
Arctic Sounds 90

CRAIG EVENSON
Waiting for You 96

POUYA RAZAVI
Echoes 98

LUCY PALMER
The Quickening 109

YVONNE HIGGINS LEACH
*We Cancel Thanksgiving Dinner After
the 2016 Election Results* 112
Walter, Wrongly Convicted 113

ALEX BOSWORTH
Summer of '76 114

JED WYMAN
Sparks 120

SKYLER MCCURINE
Black. Woman. 137

This issue is dedicated
to the memory of
JONATHAN SOBOTOR
and
SARA SCHNEIDER

MARISA CRANE

That's Why They Have Coats On

The sky to his right was a blinding white and to the left, a foreboding black. There was a strict separation between the two. The point where the two skies met could have been an arranged marriage. Awkward and forced, yet trying. Was it after their son, Nathan, the youngest of three, had been born? Had it been far earlier than that? What about when they renewed their vows a few years ago? Her tears had seemed genuine. And there was that time she had gone out with his best friend, Luke, while Jacob stayed home and graded papers. They'd ended up sleeping at Luke's and providing Jacob with an excessively long explanation as to why (he couldn't even begin to remember the details of that embarrassing creation).

He wished he could pinpoint the exact moment in which she'd given up. It would somehow allow him to compartmentalize their life together, to shelve every memory where appropriate. He looked over at her in the passenger seat. She was staring out the window at the rocky, moss-covered mountains. They stretched for miles and miles, for as far as the eye could see. Jacob knew that was a cliche saying, particularly for someone who was paid to mark them in red pen whenever he found them, but he wasn't in the business of caring much at the moment.

It had finally stopped raining in a country that had seen nothing but rain for six weeks. Jacob had secretly wanted to cancel the trip for this singular reason. He could think of better ways to spend his time than to chase Northern Lights that don't want to be found.

One sentence at a time.

That's how he was going to survive the road trip across Iceland with his ex-wife. While she wasn't technically his ex-wife—they were only separated—they had no intentions of getting back to-gether. Well, he didn't, anyway. He couldn't speak for Nadine, but he had a sneaking suspicion that the younger man he'd seen coming around the house on a semi-regular basis wasn't just a pool boy. Not that they needed a pool boy. Jacob still came around in the middle of the night and cleaned the pool when he was certain that Nadine was sleeping. It was his house, after all.

It turns out all of the movies are true: the man always moves out of his own house and gets a tiny studio apartment. The man drinks a lot of whiskey and beer at night while staring at the TV. The man keeps only milk and cheese in the fridge. The man is lactose intol-erant but now the woman is not around to bitch about his farts. The man sits in his beat-up Toyota Corolla outside the old house stuffing his face with chips and waiting to see if she's happy with the new man.

The new man, in and of himself, didn't matter much to Jacob. People go on any way that they could. This he knew. What was it their oldest daughter, Alex, had told him one night over beers? Oh yes, "The best way to get over someone is to get under someone else," or something like that. Her crassness and lack of disgust surrounding her parents' sexual exploits, he hypothesized, was a direct result of being a mere sixteen years younger than her par-ents. In the spring of his sophomore year, he could clearly recall the moment that would eventually change his life: the first domino being pushed over, if you will.

After soccer practice in the early fall, he and his buddies had been shooting the shit after showering in the locker room. It was Bob-by who had mentioned how much better he played after he had sex with his girlfriend, Brittany. He felt more at ease, calm and clear-headed. The difference was evident. The conversation then turned to Jacob and Nadine, as it so often did lately, because their one-year anniversary was coming up and that's when they had planned to have sex for the first time. When Jacob asked them about condoms, his friends assured him that Nadine wouldn't, couldn't, get pregnant her first time.

When that treacherous little plus sign materialized a few weeks later, he called her a slut and stormed out of the gas station bathroom before she could spot the tears cascading from his eyes. He returned a few minutes later offering a slurpee and Doritos as an apology. He could remember her forgiving smile that day, her head tilted, the loud sigh, the softness in her almond eyes. She assured and reassured him that he was the only one for her and always would be. Now she was fucking someone who referred to Third Eye Blind's music as "oldies."

One might wonder who in their right mind would travel to a foreign country for eleven days with their ex-whatever. Although a complete mental health assessment was not available for Jacob or Nadine, it can be said that they are generally high functioning members of society (more or less) who happen to be in a constant competition as to who can be more stubborn. Neither is aware of this competition, of course, but that doesn't seem to negate it as a legitimate way to prove superiority. Two winters ago, Jacob went the entire winter—a New England winter, mind you—without a jacket simply because Nadine had teased that he gets cold easily.

So here they were. Driving across the country to see waterfalls, volcanoes, glacier caves, anything to distract them from themselves. The flight had been pleasant enough. They'd been lucky enough to have two empty seats next to them. At one point, Nadine even laid down across three seats and fell quickly to sleep while Jacob sat upright, intermittently eyeing her with envy and reading one of many books he brought along with him. Or rather, reading and rereading the same sentence. He never could concentrate, even on things he enjoyed, when he felt unsettled.

"Some of the horses look like they're wearing wigs," he said after a particularly long period of silence.

"What?"

"You know, the brown and black horses. They have blonde manes like a drag queen that isn't fooling anyone."

She stifled a giggle.

"I don't think drag queens are *supposed* to be fooling anyone."

"Oh, for Christ's sake, you know what I mean."

"Don't the horses get cold in the rain?" Nadine tugged on her wool hat, pulling it over he ears. Jacob had scoffed at her as she waited in line at one of the git shops to pay for the overpriced garment. She had pretended not to notice.

"That's why they have coats on," he smiled.

"Now they've got wigs *and* coats, huh?"

"It's a metaphor. Their fur is longer because of the climate."

Jacob drummed his fingers on the steering wheel and wondered where thirty years had gone and whether they were really gone or had simply been misplaced.

"I don't know how I stayed married to a writer all these years," Nadine smirked, holding her hands in front of the vents, feeling for the heat.

"I'm not a writer. I'm just a lousy English professor. And you're not married to me anymore, anyway."

"By law I am. And by law, we weren't supposed to be drinking rum behind your father's farmhouse as kids either, but that didn't stop us, now did it?"

There was a lightness to her eyes when she said this. Jacob wondered if the new man ever received luminescent looks.

"Why did you feel the need to bring that up, huh? It's all in the past."

"I don't know," she said softly. "I guess I am still in the habit of telling you everything. It didn't occur to me *not* to tell you."

Jacob didn't respond. That had always been one of his favorite things about her: her unflinching honesty.

He gripped both hands tightly on the wheel, his knuckles white. The road was narrow and windy for a main road circumventing the entire country. The speed limit was 90 km per hour, which Jacob still had not converted to miles, but he knew that whatever speed it was, it felt as if he were crawling backwards through quicksand. It began to pour and the windshield wipers sped up automatically. He thought of mentioning his fascination to Nadine but he didn't have the strength.

A few hours later, Nadine was sitting on the edge of the hotel bed peeling her rain-drenched socks off of her feet. If there was a heater it would have been on full blast, but as they soon learned, Iceland did not have such things. They simply insulated the walls, which was sufficient in keeping the cold air out, but didn't provide the dreamy comfort of a toasty room.

They had both been determined to make all the stops they'd planned on the way to the southeast. Three waterfalls, a canyon, and a black sand beach, created by the ash of a nearby volcano. Of course that had meant getting out of the car and taking pictures, risking death to their smart phones. The rain wasn't violent, not like the New England rain proved to be when it lost its temper, but the frigid droplets stung their exposed skin nonetheless. Both of their faces were numb—Jacob's hands too, as he had buried his gloves deep in his suitcase, convinced they wouldn't be necessary. As they stood in cold solidarity, neither one suggested they head back to the car. They took their pictures and commented on the beauty of nature and their minute and likely pointless roles in the universe.

"It doesn't make anything we do less important though, Jake. You know?" She'd said, turning to him. Her hood was up and stray curls stuck to her face, beautifully so.

"I hate when you call me that," he said, watching the gray water cascade towards the rocks below.

"Why?"

"I have a certain fondness for the 'b' in my name."

"Oh for goodness sake, why do you always have to be so difficult? I'm just trying to talk to you, to connect."

"It's a little late for that, don't you think?"

"Fine, have it your way. Be miserable. *I'll* have a gorgeous time."

That was when he dug his foot in the gravel, aimlessly at first, then with purpose, drawing a hangman that the rain washed away before Nadine could see it.

Now he was shirtless in the bed wearing dry sweatpants and reading a book. He held the book with one hand spreading its pages like he had Nadine's lips the first time he'd performed cunnilingus on her, and cupped a glass of whiskey in the other. He'd bought it in the airport at one of those duty-free shops and relished his decision since discovering that Iceland taxed its alcoholic beverages in accordance with alcohol percentage.

Once Nadine's socks were off, she stood up and began to pull off her layers. Sweatshirt. Sweatpants. Long sleeve thermal. Leggings. T-shirt. Tank top. She walked to the bathroom in a bra and clashing underwear. Her cheeks peeked slightly out from her underwear and Jacob glanced up from his book before she disappeared from view.

Jacob heard the shower turn on and he felt compelled to join Nadine, to run his hands down her wet, naked body, to splash and play and nearly slip, to help peel her wet curls from her face, just as he had so many times before. He thought of warm baths together, of reading books and sharing a bottle of red wine on the nights that the kids went out with their friends. Nadine never did get much reading done on account of Jacob's tendency to ramble on and on about the events of *his* novel. There was rarely a filter or any sign of him picking up on social cues. Nadine displayed a great capacity for patience, although every once in awhile an indiscreet sigh would escape her mouth as she set down her book, not bothering to fold the corner of the page since she knew exactly what page she was on: the one that she had started on.

Jacob smiled, shaking his head. He knew he was difficult to be with, and maybe that's why they hadn't worked. Maybe that was why she sought refuge in the arms of a simpler man, one who wouldn't interrupt her or steal her time the way he so frequently had. He refused to believe that this man fulfilled her though, that she could wake up each day and say "I'm irrevocably happy." It simply could not be true.

The shower turned off and Nadine came out a few minutes later, holding a towel around her chest. Her hair was also wrapped in a towel and she'd missed a little mascara on her freckled face. She turned some music on and began to dance around the room. It was something he'd never heard before and before he could ask her what it was, she told him it was an Icelandic band. He was grateful that she didn't follow up that statement with, "When in Rome," or another equally as over-used phrase.

The bottle of whiskey was sitting on the nightstand next to Jacob and Nadine danced over to it, picking up and taking a long swig. He studied her as she did this.

"What? Can't you share?"

"I didn't say anything."

"It's the look on your face."

"Drink all you'd like, Nadine."

"I will." She smirked when she said this then took another swig.

Jacob put down his book and stuck his glass out. Instead of pouring him a glass, she removed the glass from his palm and set it on the nightstand.

"We are only drinking from the bottle tonight."

"Who says?"

"I do, of course. Let's forget we are some aging, semi-dignified adults for the night."

"Say no more," he said and tilted his head back and opened his mouth.

Nadine laughed and poured some whiskey down his throat.

Two hours later they were sitting on the bed together, Nadine cross-legged in pajama pants and a tank, and Jacob propped up against the headboard, still shirtless. They had been drinking steadily from the bottle as if the bottom held the secret to getting love right.

"Okay, so there's something I've always wanted to know, and I figure why the hell not ask it now. What have I got to lose?"

"What is it, dear?" He heard his voice say this term of endearment and by the time it was out of his mouth, he couldn't take it back, couldn't amend the statement.

"That woman, Christine, that used to come over for dinner sometimes."

"What about her?"

"Did you two ever, you know."

"No, I *don't* know."

"Oh, don't make me spell it out."

"Did we ever have an affair?"

"Yes. That."

"No, she's just a colleague. You know that. If I were sleeping with her, do you think I'd be so dumb as to invite her over and introduce her to you?"

"I don't *know*. Maybe it was some sort of reverse psychology thing. You never really know."

"I never cheated on you, Nadine."

"That Christine woman cut the onions wrong that one time."

He snorted so hard he nearly choked.

"What does that even mean?" he asked, once he recovered.

"Don't you remember? We were making that blue cheese cream sauce for the steaks and the onions are supposed to be sliced. She insisted upon helping so we let her cut the onions and she chopped them into microscopic pieces. Nearly ruined the sauce."

"Wow," he laughed, scratching his scruff. "Jealous much?"

She held her nose up in the air and stuck her chest out, looking as regal as she could in pajamas with pictures of cow and pig butts.

"It was simply a matter of principle. I happen to take my food preparation very seriously."

"I can see that," he said, taking a drink from the bottle before passing it to his ex-wife.

"For the record, I know you would never cheat on me. You're a good man. I just happened to have a certain distaste for that woman. I always thought she had a crush on you. *Hell*, who wouldn't have a crush on you?" She slurred the last few words and Jacob pretended not to notice. She took a sip and wedged the bottle between her thighs.

It was 1:02 A.M. and neither one was tired.

AMANDA TUMMINARO

No Smoking

Tom started puffing for a nicotine buzz.
He ignored all rules,
especially the geography of smoking.
The passing women alerted his eyesight
and grabbed at him with his blue saucers.
Tommy wanted to investigate their gutters
and read their minds and palms,
but none of them wanted to bomb their lungs.

THE STEWARDESS

The time zones divide her in to portions
and she struts through the aisle like a vision.
Her sexuality is about to bust from her bra
and she is a typical American.

She reads *Vogue* and *Allure*
and dabs her face with the suspension of a compact.
Beauty can be pulled together like a bridge,
but it can fall apart with an eye on the floor.

She's a genuine heartbreaker -
she'll eat it with her broken bread.
She's got her men in a rolodex -
When in Rome, right?

PAP SMEAR

An unfamiliar probe of twigs
by an unmerciful bastard who roams.
It's as though she has never been
in the sickening, antiseptic robe.

But she is at my feet,
my God for right now,
with fingers and utensils
to be connected to her palm.

It's a game of pursuit, and she's a king,
and I close and I close,
but the order of the power
begins to sway.

PHILIP KUAN

THE REQUEST

The request will be cleverly embedded within a popup ad which Use Case Kenny will click by accident, while surfing a dirty site. Not the type of site that you'd find bookmarked in his browser, but rather the sort a virile man would stumble upon while exploring the sponsored links of well-trusted affiliates of well-trusted affiliates of top search query results for "free streaming Asian bosoms hardcore threesome...college gone wild voyeur orgy."

Not that the aforementioned request should be tagged as porn. All it could really be accused of triggering is a discreet scrape of your contact list right before informing you, and perhaps your friends and family, of potential third parties which would repeat said scraping behavior, for nefarious shenanigans, should no action be taken. For those inclined to avoid such **#pitfalls #InevitableMisfortune #DiabolicalMachinations**, salvation awaits by clicking here. So will the request insist, with heavy font and bolding. For those who'd rather risk relationships, reputation, and mental health to the whims of an unseen global network, one possibly governed by anarchists, an option to "click here to unsubscribe" will be made available.

The request will continue its persistence with a recurring reminder, sent twice each Sunday.

An observant few might notice that the search for salvation and the request to unsubscribe inexplicably link to the same URL. Fewer will detect the additional re-scraping of their contacts, triggered by each voluntary clickthrough. However, all of this will become irrelevant, as the critical nature of the request becomes apparent.

The website itself will be filled with largely irrelevant information, except for the following blurb: "For additional questions, please contact a customer service representative during normal business hours." A phone number will be listed.

Incidentally, Use Case Kenny will circumvent the recurring reminders by programmatically filtering keywords from his inbox, thereby redirecting those threads into his spam folder, emptied weekly. Smut addicts tend to be resourceful, rather than meticulous, about the cleaning their inboxes. However, this will become irrelevant, as Use Case Kenny does not represent the request's target demographic.

Failing to unsubscribe from the mailer, Kenny's cousin Simon will fare differently. Use Case Simon will dial the support line, where an unassuming voice of feminine persuasion will engage in perfunctory conversation. The voice will be sultry while retaining its professionalism, though the content of that dialogue is irrelevant. At some point reassurances will be made that any incurred inconveniences will be remedied.

The non-aggressive lilt of her voice, which will encourage chatting on a first name basis, will assuage Simon's panic as a mildly concerning security risk within his records is unexpectedly uncovered. For verification purposes, Simon will be prompted for his home address. Briefly he might start to wonder things, but his new friend's flirtatious giggle will bring him back to the task at hand.

Following confirmation that he's been officially removed from the mailer, Simon *will* be given every opportunity to learn more about the request. Whether willing or not, his support agent will shyly suggest that they meet for coffee, to discuss it further. Simon will recall his wife's proximity to this conversation and excuse himself from the situation, using panicked intonations. By the following week, the recurring reminders will have resumed, regardless.

Simon's college roommate Jerry will fare differently. Use Case Jerry might insist upon the agent's last name, upon which the support agent will regrettably indicate that her company policy doesn't allow it. She will continue to recommend a coffee shop venue. Jerry will hesitate until he receives the photo of an attractive woman, attached to a soft copy of the request.

However, later in the day an unspecified medical emergency will prompt the support agent to cancel their appointment. Jerry will be disappointed.

A week later, a field agent identifying himself as the support agent's younger or older brother will appear, unannounced, at Jerry's front door. Regardless of Jerry's reception, the brother will make assurances that the sister's recovery is going well, before discreetly mentioning his knowledge of their budding relationship. This brother will lean in conspiratorially, to express relief that Jerry is so different from past boyfriends. Special. Refined. A stand-up chap.

Jerry will politely inform the brother that he must exit the premises. By the following week, the recurring reminders will have resumed.

Use Case Walter, Jerry's work acquaintance and fellow beta fish enthusiast, will be relieved to learn of the sister's recovery. He will welcome the brother in for a cup of tea, elated at an opportunity to learn something about his unexpected girlfriend.

Casually, the brother will ask if Walter has had opportunity to review the request during his sister's incapacitation. The brother will present a disapproving frown, upon learning that Walter has not. The brother will patiently explain that the request is not an impersonal solicitation, but a lifelong commitment, held to high standards by his passionate sister. That a request as important as this could even be said to be the key to his sister's hearth and happiness. That going forward, any half-feigned interest in the request could be detrimental to his sister's inclinations.

Walter will feel terrible, but the brother will demonstrate forgiveness.

Then, a wonderful thing will happen. Walter's resolve will steel itself, and he will insist upon reviewing the request immediately. The brother will brighten, then pull a hardcopy of the request from his briefcase. As Walter peruses the fine print there will be trembling, and wooziness, but ultimately he will make it through the manifesto with a clear understanding of what needs to be done. The brother will acknowledge Walter's recalibrated moral compass, truly worthy of his sister's cascading affection. While expressing relief at having come to the right decision, Walter will sign the contract.

A few months later, the hotly-anticipated autumn arrival of Serengeti's DP VI mid-top sneakers will reach the shelves of shoe stores nationwide. While it won't exactly capture the hearts of basketball aficionados, or redefine any aspect of the footwear industry, some critics will raise eyebrows at the pair of promotional inserts included with every online purchase.

Walter will stare at his own checkout button, resisting the urge to make that purchase. He will know full well that any attempt to recover his lost extremities will instantly void the terms of that contract, something that would cause his late betrothed to turn over in her grave. He will once again reminisce about their one and only conversation on that blustery afternoon, before shutting down his laptop.

Armed with a memory, Walter will push his wheelchair away from his desk with fewer regrets.

Click here to unsubscribe

CL BLEDSOE

SWATCHES

Everyone stop what you're doing: I want to complain
about having a house, a yard, a car, a family

that resembles one I saw in a movie, but not
the movie I wanted. My seat in the exact middle

of the theater has my name sewn in. The cushion is made
of the tears of dying mothers soaked into the finest

silk to strengthen it. I don't know who collected them
or why they were shed. Probably for love or death

or something I missed while getting popcorn. Things trudge
through the aisles bringing me candy, sodas. I've never

considered whether they have faces unless they're
cute. Mostly, I wish they'd stop breathing when I'm trying

to watch. I have an itch but my hands are drying. I have
a noise but my neck is too weak to turn. All these pizza

poppers but I'm allergic to bread, but that doesn't mean
I'll share. This movie is about the most popular woman

in the world who still can't get a job. She once
had salmon so she was fed to a grizzly. All over

the world, people reported hearing Amelia Earhart's
broadcasts for help days after she crashed. Before

she could be found, she was eaten by giant crabs.
This is what it means to try, apparently. In the lobby,

a man offers swatches from a line of ties he's hoping
to sell across the world. They are the best ties,

he's sure of it. For each one sold, a child is taught
a lesson in dream deferment. I see people trading
their tickets to buy just one. But I have to return
to my seat before the trailers end.

Telling the White Man a Secret

The tune your mother sang before you learned that life is more
about caesura than song.
The color of her eyes, the sky in spring when the dying is done.
The color of her eyes, the grass, growing to feed the multitudes.
The color of her eyes, the deepest loam which is life.

The smell of hair, subtle sweat and vanilla.
A breeze tipsing through the tall grass.
A thousand spears stabbing feet, dark sap for blood.

Mumbling in the corner, outside the door.
Even darkness isn't empty.
A laugh from the street. A car thunders awake. Sleep is something
for other people to worry about.

Bloom where you're fertilized. Fingers clenched tight to protect the
soft palm.
Bloom when you learn to unclasp, to reach, to take something
other than yourself,
your own fear, into your palm.
Bloom when you can, if you can remember what it is to feel the
sun.

Magic is another word for exhaustion.
Love is a way of weeping, forever, of never weeping again.

You'll never see her again until your mind breaks.
Even then, you won't remember where you left the box of feathers
she gave you.
Can you imagine how long it took her to catch the birds she took
them from?

When the white man comes, tell him the greatest secret, which is
that he knows everything
and nothing, he is everything and nothing.

With the Old Magazines and Spiders

Will there be more ages than this? Or will
the years drop off into gold-plated rot?

Aliens from the future will know our remains
by the smell. Don't worry. They've got a pill

for everything except having trouble
swallowing. It's tiring, all this being right

when no one cares about the truth. I don't
want to keep yelling at the wind for the cost

of repairing my windows. It just wants to get
in out of the cold; it's not smart enough

to know it can't actually feel. But letting it
in means there'll be nothing but in. The same

is true of the mistakes of history, which
we've chosen to wear around our wrists

like the finest woven hairs of our long-dead
childhood friends. I'm kidding. We never had

childhoods. Heads bowed in the dark, we were
always too old to laugh at fat people falling

down stairs, monkeys smoking cigars. How
to reconcile love of people and fear of what

they do? The aliens, do you think they'll be
entertained? Or just file us away in a dusty attic?

THE BEAN KING

Riding my bike through an imaginary world of pianos hovering
on ledges hoping the breeze remains at my back. I cross
at the light while distracted bus drivers speed through. This

is what happens when people ask questions: someone
is inconvenienced. Even white men die alone
but are eaten by the finest worms, believe me. All blood is red

unless it's blue. All blood splatters, turns black
with time. The only reason I know is because I've bled before.
Believe me.

***

Each day, we feast, each night, we sleep deep and dream
that outside, there's nothing but the greenest leaves,

the bluest skies. The hint of smoke never penetrates
our state-of-the-art filters, and if it did, we'd sue.

The problem with infinity is that someone's always trying
to end it. They don't understand how hard it is. The milk

sours, the honey sets. Bedsores are a concern, as is boredom.
Just be glad the walls are see-through. Maybe someday

your children will taste the air inside the doorway
if you're willing to give up the best days of your life.

My grandparents built those mines, used the proceeds to build
this wall, so don't tell me I don't know the value of hard work.

NICOLE MARTINEZ
Worlds Apart

Pluto hovered through the darkness, making a beeline for the other dwarf planets. From this angle, it was nearly impossible to see Pluto's familiar heart-shaped birthmark; it was shrouded in darkness. Pluto's expression was just as dark, glum and distraught. If it were possible, it would have seemed as though Pluto was crying.

The planet came to a halt in front of his friends, trying to hide his obvious agitated state of mind, but it was no use. The dwarf planets glided to his side.

"What's wrong?" Ceres asked at Pluto's approach.

"They kicked me out!" wailed the dwarf planet. "They say I can't be one of them anymore. I'm no longer a planet. I'm just a puny dwarf!" At this, Pluto paused, realizing that he might have offended his friends. But they were more concerned with providing him support.

"There, there," consoled Haumea as she bobbed in Pluto's direction. Despite being dwarfed by Pluto herself, Haumea had maternal instincts, and the others looked toward her lead in this unexpected situation. But Pluto remained inconsolable.

"At least you had 76 years with the big guys—that's more than any of us had," chimed in Makemake, trying to sound reassuring and not at all jealous. It wasn't working, and the others glanced in his direction. Makemake was the most recent to have joined the group, and he wasn't yet familiar with planetary politics.

Eris, especially, didn't think this was the angle they should use to try to cheer up their friend. "Anyway, ignore those big bullies. They call us cold but, damn, they're the frigid ones!"

"Yeah!" echoed the others, all except Ceres, in chorus. Ceres remained quiet, having yet to make a peep since Pluto's return. Ceres had been nearer to the sun than any of the other planets, and she was more accustomed to the dynamic of the solar system. She wouldn't be roped into yet another circular discussion

"I guess you're right," replied Pluto. "Yeah, yeah, you guys are right! And you know what? I sometimes got the feeling that those guys were talking about me when I wasn't around. I mean, who does that?" Pluto's dejected feeling gave way to righteous anger, and the rest of the group was happy enough for the change. They were glad for the change of tone, despite its negativity.

Only Ceres held back, ruminating over her words before speaking. "There's no use in being upset. Things change, but still, we turn and we dance around the sun. Whatever they might think of us doesn't matter. It changes nothing."

The space around the dwarf planets became even more hushed, with nothing but Pluto's sniffles in the background while the other dwarf planets felt guilt in response to Ceres' admonishment. They were ashamed by their hasty words. How could planets so far from the sun be so hot-headed?

Eris felt only a twinge of guilt. She was fed up with being treated as though she was less than the other planets, and Pluto's return and response to being rebranded as a dwarf planet stung. Even one of their own thought being a dwarf planet wasn't good enough. Eris, however, held her tongue.

Haumea broke the silence with soft tones. "We missed you, dear one." The others seemed to nod in agreement with this sentiment.

"We did!" exclaimed Makemake as he bobbed excitedly in front of Pluto. "It seemed like you were gone forever. I wasn't sure if I was ever going to see you again, and forever is such a very long time!" The childlike planet became downcast, but quickly forgot his sadness. "Anyway, you must have seen and heard a lot of things!

That's why you were so busy, isn't it? Tell us all about it!"

An excited buzz moved through the group, as Pluto prepared to regale them with his tales.

"You're right. It was quite exciting. So much has happened. I don't know where to start. I guess I forgot to mention my visitor!"

"A visitor?!" Makemake couldn't contain his excitement, and even Eris seemed interested. Ceres was no stranger to visits, however, and was less impressed.

"Yes. This tiny machine buzzed by me twice, like a bug. I almost missed it the first time, but then it returned."

"Was it scary?" Haumea wondered out loud. She didn't like the sound of it.

"Not at all, Haumea. Don't you worry. It simply snapped my photo, so I tried to show off my best side. But you know how it is. Sometimes you get all turned around."

"Where do you think it came from?" asked Makemake, who was enthralled with Pluto's story.

"I'm not sure," Pluto admitted nonplussed. "But it kept going past me. Maybe some of you saw it?" The dwarf planets chattered among each other, wondering if they had missed something exciting while their friend was gone.

"I didn't see your visitor, but I've noticed activity myself. Something has been popping in and out of my periphery for a while now, but I didn't want to excite the rest of you." Ceres' reticence to make this admission was apparent, but Makemake was far too excited to take note. He felt as though he might burst, but that would have been a very bad idea indeed.

"Wow! What do you think they're doing? Will someone visit me, I wonder? I hope so!" A murmur went through the crowd. They were being infected by little Make's enthusiasm, who was now trying—and failing—to peek around Ceres to get a glimpse of this thing. Still, Ceres was cautious.

"They come from the little blue planet, Earth." Ceres conjectured. "Third from the Sun. Not nearly as grandiose as Jupiter or Saturn. Just a single moon, Luna." Ceres didn't let on that this moon was bigger than any of them.

She continued, "Yet, there's always something going on there. Once, they even sent something from the surface of Earth to Charon. And things orbit around the planet." Ceres paused to collect her thoughts. "It's hard to keep track. Tiny constructs have moved through space from Earth to Mars, but they're like nothing I've seen before. And now they're visiting us. I don't know if this is good."

"Surely it can't be bad," mused Haumea, ever the optimist. Her mind was already birthing fantastic possibilities about the tiny machines that were roaming the solar system, having forgotten her earlier hesitance.

"Yeah, my visitor only whizzed passed twice. I'm no worse for the wear." Pluto wasn't ready to accept that these were bad omens. Besides, it was the only positive he had going for him, and he was in no state to resign himself to a life devoid of any perks.

"Still, we should be careful," argued Ceres. "We don't know what it means. We've spent years out here on our own, and this sudden activity could mean bigger things are coming. We just don't know, and those planets won't tell us anything."

At this, Eris was ready to enter into the conversation again, still seething from the furor of before. "They probably know exactly what it means but won't tell us just because we're dwarf planets! It's just like them. They hog all the warmth of the sun, and now they hog the news, too!"

"I don't really know if they're any wiser than we are..." Pluto's mumble trailed off. He wasn't sure he was ready to defend the planets. He was doubtful that they had ever really accepted him now that he'd been given the boot, even if there weren't all involved in some conspiracy against the outer planetoids. Still, Eris was so quick to judge.

"Well, we may not know what they know, but I can tell you what I know." Haumea sounded as though she wanted to avoid encouraging Eris' anger anymore.

"Yeah, what's that?" grumbled Eris, who felt slighted that the rest of the dwarf planets weren't agreeing with her.

"We all missed you, Pluto. I, for one, am glad you're back." Pluto couldn't help but melt at Haumea's motherly tone, and the other dwarf planets chimed in with similar sentiments.

"I'm so glad you've returned!"

"We worried you had forgotten about us!"

"Never!" Pluto protested.

Makemake flitted quickly between the only family he'd ever known, still abuzz and happy that everyone seemed to be getting along for once. Even Ceres seemed to bob in closer, closing the space between Pluto and herself. At least these guys still accepted Pluto.

"But we've got work to do," came the gentle reminder from motherly Haumea.

Slowly, the dwarf planets parted ways, returning to their own orbits. Makemake twirled off into his lane, and Ceres spun back into place among the larger planets. The other planets followed suit, and Pluto seemed to rotate wistfully in his orbit, feeling once again connected to the dwarf planets.

Pluto faced toward the larger eight planets until he slowly turned away, his view obscured by darkness. Maybe it wasn't so bad simply being a planetoid object. Still, it had been nice while it lasted.

KEVIN MCCOY

ocean – kyle of tongue

we were young and we pulled over and
we saw the ocean as vast as a
mythological monster.

sculpted cliffs like the bones
of some slowly dying leviathan of rock
stripped of flesh.

the long tongue of the kyle creeping closer
to the stony crags embraced in
 biting clouds of frozen mist.

how dumb the human heart
human thought
human fate
naked before the place where
time was born.

how small is being
beneath its infinite face.

a soft foot fall
in the uncountable sands swept
by ocean.

CAT DIXON
Women in the Workplace

Feel the pressure as if someone is pressing on the back of your eye-
ball to make it pop out like the pushing down of a seat belt release,
liberating the belt's metal tongue, like pushing on an elevator's
button, waiting for the ding, and the doors open to take you to the
bottom floor, the foyer, so you can stroll across the lobby, breeze
through the automatic doors, and walk to your car, throw your
bag inside, slam your butt in the leather seat, and drive home to
someone
else who dictates what the rest of your life will be.

BRETT MORRIS

I Wanted to be a Hero

I always wanted to be a hero. I wanted to be the one who took care of business when others couldn't or wouldn't step up to the plate. I was always hoping that something would happen; someone would need rescuing so I could be a hero. But until that day, I thought I would never get the chance.

It started as an ordinary day by the harbor. The sun was shining and the air was fresh and clear. My wife and I were sitting on a bench eating lunch when it happened. A large object came screaming out of the sky and landed in the harbor with a mighty splash. The waves spread out quickly, coming over the embarcadero railing and swamping the area in dirty seawater. Some people were knocked down by the wave. Everyone was taken by surprise by the commotion. All was still and quiet for a moment as the surprise set in. As the object bobbed to the surface and settled itself down it became apparent what it was; a giant Alien spaceship. When they realized what it was, all the people panicked. Terror gripped them and they ran for their lives. They didn't know what was in the craft or what would happen. But I knew.

It was Them. They had finally come to take over Earth. I had found out about their plans for invasion. Looking through my telescope and listening to my interstellar radio I knew it was coming; I just didn't know when. I knew they wanted to enslave us to run their semprini farms, so I had prepared for this day. I had my Tweetzer with me, so I took it out of its holster and headed for the harbor's edge. Everyone else was running away in blind panic and fear, but not me. I was running to Them. My only chance to defeat Them was to get to their craft before they could get out and open fire. I had to get to Them while they were still inside their ship; when they were at their most vulnerable.

A panicked tourist ran his boat into the dock at the fish restaurant and fled up the ladder to run inland. Before the boat could careen away I jumped down into it and rammed the throttle forward. I pointed the boat directly at the big space ship and charged at it watching for the opening hatch; hoping I could get to them before they came out. As I got closer, I climbed onto the bow of the speeding boat, ready to jump as soon as I got there. Just as the boat crashed into the spacecraft, I saw the hatch was opening and a slimy tentacle reached out for a grab handle. Wasting no time, I leapt off the boat and ran swiftly up the sloping side, reaching the hatch just as the first alien head popped out.

Aiming more by instinct than intent, I raised my Tweetzer and blasted it right in the middle of its many eyes. It made a high pitched scream and fell back into the open hatch. Reaching the hatch, I kicked it open with my foot and pointed my weapon down into the spacecraft and started blasting. Screams of pain and terror came out of the craft as I rained death on them. After emptying the first magazine, I reloaded and started down into the spacecraft. Carefully looking left and right, I searched every chamber of the craft dodging the blasts of their deadly Ph'tangs.

It was chaos inside the spaceship. Shrapnel from blasts that hit bulkheads and equipment was flying everywhere. Sparks rained down on me from electronics shorting out from the destruction; the floors were slick with their blood. I blasted away at anything that moved until finally, I had the Alien leader cornered.

"Puny human," the leader snarled. "You may have defeated us but more will come and we will take over your planet. You will work our semprini farms for us just like a thousand other planets do."

"Not on my watch Ickblatz! You'll never conquer Earth."

"Gasp! You know my name. How can that be?"

"I'm onto you and your planet's schemes. I've been listening to your transmissions with my Illudium Q-38™ interstellar radio. I know everything. By the way, your wife is banging the semprini delivery man while you're away."

"What! It can't be. Fllaaaaaaaaaall is unfaithful? No, I don't believe it. You lie, puny Human."

"True story, bro."

"Bah! It doesn't matter. More will come, you'll see."

"If they dare show their faces here, they'll get blasted to smithereens, just like you will. You can't win against us; we're tough and resourceful."

"Shazbat," it replied, "bested by an Earthling."

It was the last thing he said, because I blasted him just like I had blasted all the other aliens. As his dying shriek faded away, their spacecraft no longer echoed with the screams of dying aliens. I had killed the lot.

Finally, shaking from the adrenaline rush, I climbed out of their now lifeless spacecraft and signaled the Navy that all was clear. Although I was covered with alien blood and entrails, the sailors took me straight to their headquarters for debriefing. Admiral McGinty himself shook my hand and thanked me for being so resourceful. He told me his sailors were prepared to fight Communists, not an alien invasion and things would have been bad if not for A Real Hero like me.

The city threw me a ticker tape parade. "Our Hero!" the banners proclaimed. The Italian actress Gina Lolapalooza, the most beautiful woman in the world, told me she wanted to have my baby. The famous artist Salvador Wally made a sculpture of me, and the mayor said it will have a place of honor in front of City Hall. The President came to town and personally thanked me and asked me what I would like to do with myself.

"I want to live a quiet and peaceful life," I said, "but as long as they are out there we can't afford to be complacent. I want to teach our military how to fight Them, so that when they come back, we'll be better prepared to take them on."

"I will make it so," the President proclaimed.

Then my wife elbowed me in the ribs. "Stop daydreaming," she said, "you'll spill your drink."

***

Meanwhile on Epsilon 5, Ickblatz was wasting time on the company computer. His life was so boring, that the only thing that gave him any enjoyment was the game, "Invasion Earth." The problem was, he couldn't get past level 3. He couldn't figure out how to get past the plucky Earthling who always seems to outsmart him. "Harumph," he thought, as his character expired for the tenth time. Then his thoughts were interrupted by his name being shouted at him.

"Ickblatz! Are you playing that damn game again? Stop daydreaming and get back to work. Those semprini deliveries aren't going to happen by themselves."

Grumbling a few non-specific curses directed at his boss, Ickblatz closed the game and opened up the company page. Seeing a call-waiting icon on his screen, he clicked on it and when the line picked up said, "Semprini Amalgamated, Ickblatz speaking, may I have your order please?"

KATHLEEN LANGSTROTH

Primary Education

Finalist for the 2017 So Say We All Literary Prize in Fiction

Walk past the first panel of bricks, one concrete divider, second panel of bricks, second concrete divider, two steps over. There. Back to wall, one foot up against the brick wall. About five minutes. Crouch down for another five, return to standing for the last five. The bell will signal the end.

The learning institution. Most of it is forgotten as memory prioritized adult concerns. But here and now, I cope with my carefully composed worries. Their organic quality helps them grow each day. Near my right foot, there is a smooth long white stone embedded in the pavement. It is surrounded by some more grey stones and many black lumps that have white speckles on them. I stand with the same array each recess. I study the stone and brick and concrete until people disappear. Almost.

Here comes a group of eight girls. They encircle me against the wall and first sing, then yell, a lilting and taunting song that instructs me to join their group or get kicked by the entire ensemble before the song ends. I do not join. They all kick me half-heartedly and move off. My eyes tear up again. It would have been simpler to join. I remain still.

A bell. Time to file in. Line up here. Lots of pushing and one elbow in the side. In a mass, I am not singled out which is preferable. Almost comfortable. Invisibility is ideal. March into the building, up three stairs, along the rubber entry mat through wire-meshed glass doors that no one holds open. Bump into the edge of the door. Lot of yelps and giggles and 'Heys' in close proximity as we move together into the hallway leading to classrooms. Boots off and against the wall. Drooping socks drag along the smooth, slippery floors with a thin layer of dried mud and dust. Into the back of my first grade class to hang my coat on a long wire rack with black, block capital letters on peeling, crusty masking tape indicating my designated place. Take a seat.

To a desk that wobbles against the others. This group of four includes two desks that are higher by one and a half inches...I mean about five centimetres, we have to convert now. The wood-splintered chair back catches on my sweater as I slide into my seat. I can tell someone swapped this chair. Yesterday, my seat didn't wobble or catch my clothes. I avoid getting a sliver from this wooden slab perched on its hollow metal tubing frame and pull in my chair. The rubber feet make that funny honk noise as I move forward.

I really need to get home.

We have been told to complete a page in our journal. This task involves filling up an entire page in a half-sized notebook. Date at the top. One sentence at the bottom. "Today is a cloudy day." I need to illustrate this so I add a simple stick-type figure with a purple triangle dress. Brown straight sticks indicate my long brown hair. (I can nearly sit on it now.) Black crayon dashes fall from blacker ballooning clouds. On sunny days, I can alter this to white ballooning clouds and the standard yellow circle with protruding sticks for rays. My minimum effort will result in one large satisfying red check mark later this morning. I have to stay here all day. Pace yourself.

I really need to get home.

Today, I need to take the attendance folder down to the office with another girl. I like to be chosen by the teacher. The girl with me has strange black, horn-rimmed glasses and is far too pleased with everything. I don't like her but I can't think that way. It only makes things difficult. She insists that we be friends and hold hands. She insists that we detour to the girls' washroom. This is a conflict. I don't want to displease her. She is my friend because she says she is and she pulls me along the hallway. I can't have her hate me. But I know Miss Murray wants me to go directly to the office and deliver this folder. I need to get this girl on my side. I don't even know where the office is in this huge building. Everything appears to be a great distance from me and threatens to swallow up my smallness. The tasks involved in surviving school become increasingly more complicated each hour. I don't see a choice. I go to the bathroom.

We enter to mocking echoes and pungent ammonia scent. A thin line of windows high up the wall cast a sickly green light on the pale blue concrete tomb. I gauge my options. I don't see any so I stay rooted to the floor near the entrance to the bathroom. We won't stay long. She plays with the giant sink. A sculptural creation made from the same polished tile and concrete aggregate that seems to form the whole building. This is a group sink, much like a circular trough that has a ten foot radius and dazzles its users as it sprinkles water like an ornamental palace fountain. Rounded edges to comfortably lean in on. A corresponding circular foot pedal surrounds the bottom of the sink so that any child can turn on the hundreds of fine strands of water. The resulting friendly trickling liquid sound contrasts nicely with the abrupt clunking of the foot pedal. My friend is slamming the pedal repeatedly to test the utilitarian attributes of this wonder sink. School is supposed to be about learning and exploring and discovering and socializing. Isn't it?

I really think that we need to go.

Eventually, we do arrive at the office where Vicky (apparently) abruptly and with a flourish, presents the attendance folder to the harassed secretary of perhaps eighty years. I know immediately that she hates me and loves this sweet girl with massive smile and her delivery of important statistical information. At her suggestion and with a wisp of rebelliousness, we skip back to class where happily, Miss Murray has not yet become suspicious in regards to what must be our lengthy absence. Monitor the clock.

A busy morning ahead. We need to visit the library. This is a sweet relief to me. A place of refuge where nothing is expected of you.

Simply sit quietly and this woman presents all of us with a large hard-covered book with stiff plastic taped over its paper sleeve for protection. The aged librarian licks her fingers before she turns each thick yellowed page. Maybe she can be my real friend. She shares this story despite the fact that some audience members clearly don't deserve it. Boys try to toss dead leaves at each other from the carpeted floor. Giggling girls play with each other's hair. I allow the girl behind me to attempt to braid my hair. What else am I going to do? The story is about a big old wooden house that needs painting. There are some disagreements about colour choices. The resulting conflict ends with all the colours somehow getting splashed onto the house. Incredibly, the house turns out to be painted white because when you mix all of these colours, you get white! Quite a revelation if you ask me. And now we get to stand up and browse the shelves so that we can take home a book. What an incredible opportunity.

File through the hallways to allow for a quick survey of other classrooms and doorways to outside freedom. Back at class, it's time to deal with the usual routine. I must smile and listen to everything my best friend says. She sits opposite me and lives in a house opposite to mine on the street. I cannot avoid her. Ever. She carefully passes me a note encoded: MTW 10. This means the pending spelling dictation test must be altered to receive a poor mark. Out of twenty words, I must only receive ten red check marks. So, thinking as quickly as I can, I must spell the words I think are correct and then go back and turn ten of them into errors. After all, this is a dictation. Time is a consideration. I must follow these instructions with every assignment each day, every day. Ensure the ruse will fool the teacher indefinitely. This is forever I think. I am so tired.

I really need to get home.

Lunch does miraculously arrive. I get ready quickly so that I can perhaps walk home alone. She is popular and talks and laughs with others. She is busy. I leave the room without notice. I am out the door. In a blur of agonized hope and glory, I move away from everyone. As though I have forgotten that I must return this afternoon and everyday through the school year. And more after that. Never mind. Focus on moving forward right now. Faces rush by, voices exploding but none seem directed to me. Slipping away from bodies and sounds. Around the corner of the brick edifice to leave. We are all just children. We are all the same. Out of the line of sight from most of them, I pick up my pace. Freedom for one hour. Half a day gone. No one speaks to me.

This is my hour.

I am walking home now.

I am running home now. And more after that.

TONI MARTIN

Fool's Gold

Finalist for the 2017 So Say We All Literary Prize in Fiction

Once, when I was a little girl, Mama let slip that a beautiful woman killed her brother. I have been wheedling the story out of her ever since.

I never knew Charlie. The tragedy occurred before I was born. Or maybe the year that I was born. She can't remember.

"Were you pregnant at the funeral?" I ask, in the kitchen, where I corner her. We are cooking dinner together as we used to, wearing our aprons, except now she is helping me in my house. The apron she has borrowed from me is too long. I have grown up and she has shrunk.

"I can't remember," she repeats, cutting a carrot directly into the pot on the stove, the knife aimed at her thumb. Her fingers are puny and her knuckles are as big as Tootsie Roll Pops. I chop cucumber for the salad on a cutting board.

I have only been pregnant once, and every day was symbolic. Mama was pregnant five or six times (she can't remember) counting the miscarriages, so it all runs together.

"What difference does it make if I was pregnant? " she asks impatiently. "My brother died." After the carrots, she chops potatoes into the stew, and fills a pot with water for rice. She makes rice for every dinner because she grew up with it. The cook in my grandparents' house in Savannah was a Geechee woman from the Sea Islands.

I risk another question.

"How old was he when he died?"

"Young."

"In his twenties?"

She thinks. "No. Thirties, I guess. I don't remember. I don't want to remember." Don't make me remember, she means.

In our family, like yours, pain and truth are two streams of an underground river, impossible to separate.

Charlie was Mama's younger brother. Her only brother. Boys were favored in those days, make no mistake. The man was the boss. As a child, I visited my grandfather's house in Savannah and saw for myself. In the daytime, the women scurried about, shelling crab and polishing the mahogany furniture, preparing for the moment when Grandpa arrived home from work. They waited on him, fed him and left him alone in the parlor, to smoke his cigar and drink a shot of bourbon in peace.

With my father it was much of a muchness. I am the middle of three girls, less of a disappointment than the third, but a disappointment nonetheless. We played and chattered until he arrived, then we served him. He did not answer the telephone himself and if we forgot to put out the salt at dinner, he surveyed the table and said, "Pass the salt, please," so that one of us had to get up. He never put us to bed or bought us a gift. We were Mama's job. Our job was to keep quiet and out of his way, our hair braided, the piano closed. When my father died, I felt that I expanded from two dimensions into three. Maybe an uncle, an uncle who looked for beauty, would have seen it in us girls, too.

I can imagine how Charlie lived, with his family, and even when he went to college, because he stayed in a house with my grandmother and his cousins. It was the nineteen thirties. Each fall, from the time the oldest started high school, Grandma moved the household up to Columbus, Ohio so that the children could get a "decent education" in the public schools. My grandparents did not share the definition of decency that was current in Savannah.

Grandpa stayed behind to run his businesses: a bank, a life insurance company, a mortuary and a movie theatre. He had his corner of Savannah covered.

In this way, all four children and several cousins finished high school and Ohio State University. No one lived in a dormitory or mingled with outsiders. My grandmother hired a woman in Columbus to help her cook and clean house. The children were to study. The girls did and remained diligent all their lives. But not Charlie and the boy cousin D. J. Grandma sent D.J.home after he painted a neighbor's house unbidden.

Charlie was the only boy left, bored in a house of good girls. Columbus was cold compared to Savannah. Liquor warmed a fellow, all right. At night he roamed the clubs and the juke joints. I imagine he listened to the blues and the boogie-woogie, because I love them so, and it has to come from somewhere.

They say that he was handsome and I believe it. I have not seen photographs of him as a man, only as a boy, slim and fresh. When I was a girl and first saw the pictures, I imagined playing with him, forgetting that he was a man when he died. With his family, he looks serious. His hair is slicked back but there is a wave to it that the pomade does not suppress. My mother beside him is clear-eyed and serene, like a princess. The family is all dark-haired and dark-eyed, like me. You might say they look Jewish, or Latin, but you'd be wrong.

When the romance began, Charlie was in law school and the youngest cousin, Liz, was in college along with Mama's younger sister. All at Ohio State, in Columbus, living with Grandma. Mama had graduated, married a year later and moved to Detroit, so she was not an eye witness. Liz lives in Florida now, with her third husband, the Sweetheart. Over the phone, I ask her the same questions I ask Mama, but every answer is different.

I met Liz when I was ten. She grew up in Manhattan and attended The Ethical Culture School before Ohio State. She gushes like a

New Yorker. "What a darling outfit!" I had never heard an adult speak with exclamation points before. She and Mama are the last ones standing.

Liz wore "pumps" and "hose," not shoes and stockings, to work. She taught me the color "taupe" and the concept "career woman." Mama says Liz stayed slim because she never had children, in a tone that suggests that Liz was the lucky one.

One night, in a smoky after hours place, Charlie saw the woman he should not have seen. Ora. Her hair was chestnut with red high-lights. She had fair skin and gray green eyes. There are no pictures of her either, but everyone old enough to know her marveled that she was the child of her parents, who were no handsomer than you and me. Liz says that Ora's mother was white trash. Her father was a light-skinned Negro who ran the numbers game in the colored neighborhood. I picture a dandy in a pin-striped suit with wide lapels. Every day the horses ran, he strutted down Long Street, Ora on his arm, his German Shepherd at his heels. When he won big, he bought his beautiful daughter a new hat.

In the kitchen, I tell my mother what I learned about Ora.

"Who told you that?" She wheels on me, knife in hand, forgetting that Liz is the only one left.

"What?" But it has to be about color, to make her so angry.

"Ora's mother wasn't white." She says that Ora's mother was light enough to pass, as they were, but colored all the same.

"And did you pass, in Columbus?" I have her trapped. If she tries to leave, the rice may burn. I may let it burn. "Did Ohio State know that you were Negroes?"

"They knew."

"How did they know? Did you tell them, did they ask your race when you registered?"

"We never lied."

I never thought that they lied. My mother stayed with her mother, always her parents' daughter, until she was her husband's wife. She was never in the world, as I am, to have to consider lying. I lie when I do not speak, when I let white people assume, Jewish or Latin. White is the polite color, the one that does not cause trouble. My husband is white, and he is impatient when I speak up.

"What difference does it make?" he says. He means now. White people always mean now.

Maybe he is right. I used to think it was important, whether Ora was all colored or mixed. I figured that if she were part white, that would explain the discontent that plagued her, later, as a wife. All these years I have tried to discover the truth of the matter. Yet, if you turn the story over as much as I have, you can see that she was the same color, whatever she was called. Her skin may have been sprinkled with fine freckles, like mine, or it may have been creamy smooth, like Mama's. Charlie thought she was beautiful and he was lost.

Was Ora a student? No one seems to know. If she was, she didn't need to be. Her smile was enough accomplishment. The couple courted all over the city. Ora found Charlie on campus and slipped her hand into his. They kissed by the Scioto River, and looked across the water. At night, downtown, they met at the clock tower of the Lazarus department store, garlanded in lights. And returned to the clubs, where she hung on his arm, sparkling.

Mama never visited a club. I asked her what she did for fun in Columbus, but she doesn't remember. Charlie lived a different life, because he was a man, a life as remote to his sisters as a fairytale. Mama wanted to be out in the world, but she wanted to be a good girl more. They told her, when she graduated, that there was no call for a colored girl who spoke French. She gave Charlie the proxy for her dreams, gave it freely, assuming, from loyalty, that he would vote her mind and stay the course.

It was an unsettled time in Columbus. The Klan rode out at night in the Ohio countryside. There were rumors of new conflict in Europe. My grandfather's bank closed, so Charlie had less pocket money. But Prohibition was over, and Charlie and Ora had each other. He declared his intention to marry her.

"He was a fool," Mama says.

Love makes you foolish, I think.

Charlie's mother, in Columbus, met Ora before his father did. If Grandma objected to Ora's face paint and fluttery ways, she said nothing. Charlie was her son, the favorite. She must have been worried about what her husband would say, though. Did she tell him before or after Charlie's grades started to fall?

Charlie flunked a course. No one in the family had ever flunked a course. Mama was Phi Beta Kappa. Liz says, "You can't imagine your grandmother's dismay." But I can imagine. I am a mother, too. And I knew my grandparents, the stern businessman and the dutiful wife. They would have told themselves that Charlie's grades didn't matter if he passed the Bar exam. To Charlie, everything was optional except Ora.

Ora's mother came to the wedding in a housedress. She was that low class.

Did Ora love Charlie? "Yes," Liz says. "No," Mama says. They agree that Ora wanted to escape Columbus, to see the world. Charlie took her home to Savannah, which was not what she expected. She knew that Charlie's father owned many businesses. She did not understand why Charlie had to work his way up in his own father's company. Charlie did not pass the bar examination. Few Negroes did in those days, what did nigras need lawyers for? Yet grandfather took it hard.

The couple lived with Charlie's parents, where silence was the rule. No boogie-woogie in that dark parlor. I imagine them in the bedroom off the back stairs, as far as possible from Grandpa and Grandma's bedroom up front. There used to be a four poster bed there, made up with lace-trimmed white sheets, and a white chenille bedspread, like a bed in museum. I imagine a Saturday morning. The sun is high and hot and they've missed breakfast. No reason to leave the shady room, where the heat is theirs and the clotted sheets absorb the wet. They wake, they doze. The ceiling fan revolves.

Later, Ora sits at the dressing table, the one with the mirror in the middle and marquetry drawers on both sides. Her hair lifts and frizzes in the heat, redder than ever, on fire. Charlie, behind her, breathes in her dense perfume and makes faces in the mirror, the way his mother did for us. Ora laughs a deep laugh of contentment that her in-laws never hear. Charlie takes the hairbrush from her hand and brushes the fierce hair until it settles down. Ora applies pomade lightly, for shine, and Charlie continues to brush, with long, smooth strokes. She closes her eyes, hypnotized.

Ora had to live colored in the South, eyes cast down, which did not suit her, even if she was all colored and maybe she wasn't. I feel sorry for her, if she had to learn the rules suddenly, as a wife. I learned the rules as I grew, so they crippled me gently, the way a bound foot shortens. It was painful but no one talked about it because that it had to be. Ora was unbound.

She convinced Charlie to leave, to take a job in Dayton. She said that the South suffocated her, that they could only be themselves again, in love, in the North. Once they returned to Ohio, she ran away to Columbus. Lovesick, he pursued her. Liz says he would have done anything for her, even break off from the family and live white in the North.

Could Charlie have crossed over, with all the family's light focused on him? Mama would say "no," so I don't ask her. Grandpa's brothers did it. Mama and Charlie grew up without their uncles, knew the cost of passing. It was as though the uncles had died. There were cousins, but Mama only saw them once. And now it is like they never existed. We don't even know their names. At least we remember Charlie.

Ora would not come back to Dayton. Then she would not talk to Charlie. The beaus that she had left behind swirled around her like tentacles and swallowed her up. Charlie slunk away. Eventually they divorced. What else could he do?

He returned home, still the family's hope, though tarnished. He worked for his father. In a few years, he remarried, a trim brown-skinned woman six years older than he was. She was a nurse, pretty in a quiet way, and she took care of him. She wore no make up. I knew her long after he died, when she was the darkest aunt, and solemn.

Some months after the wedding, Charlie visited Liz in New York. He drank too much, and used four letter words in front of her. "He was not himself," she says. The way her voice breaks, these fifty years later, I believe that she loved him as much as Mama did, and maybe not like a brother. I have come to consider that love settles variously, like water. Sometimes light reflects off the surface, and we wade in from the shore. People see us and smile. Other times, we jump into a dark pool, too deep, when no one is looking. The water closes silently over our heads.

Charlie drank too much in Savannah, also, but not in front of his wife. In the bars. One night, on the way home, he drove into a tree. When the ambulance picked him up, they thought he was white, and took him to the white hospital. At the hospital, they went through his wallet and recognized his name. They put him back in the ambulance and transferred him to a colored hospital.

Mama says that he might have lived, if they had kept him at the white hospital. Liz says that he still might have lived, at the colored hospital, but his wife, the nurse, had him transferred again, to a better colored hospital. I suspect that a man with severe internal injuries from an auto accident didn't have much of a chance in Savannah in the early fifties, at any hospital. But the way it happened, bitterness lodged in every heart.

"Come set the table, Rose," my mother calls to my daughter. She has hazel eyes and red-brown hair with gold highlights. Mama says beauty is a curse. I say beauty is a gift and I tell Rose the same.

I have asked Mama and Liz what happened to Ora, but they don't know.

"We didn't keep up with her," Mama says, lips tight. I hope that if Ora is alive, that she is not alone, and not bitter.

Rose swings through the door. Mama is silent.

People say that Rose looks like me. How can that be, since I was not beautiful? I wish I could see myself at thirteen again, with my new spherical eyes.

"What's wrong, Grandma ?" Rose asks, looking at me.

"Your mother wants me to tell her fairy tales. Even you are too old for fairy tales." Mama shakes out the dish towel and hangs it up.

That is not what I want, not what I ever wanted. I want the truth, and the pain, too, if that is the truth. I want both streams, the whole river, to run free aboveground in a wide, bright channel.

Rose puts her arm around my waist and speaks for me, to Mama. "There are grown up fairy tales, Grandma. You can tell, because they have a sad ending."

artwork by Laura Gwynne

DAVID HENSON

THE TINDER MEN

Winner of the 2017 So Say We All Literary Prize in Fiction

Alice spends her mornings searching Tinder for men who look like they might bring weed. She makes plans to meet at a bar of their choosing, then stops responding to their texts for the rest of the day. An hour after she's supposed to meet the men she says, Sorry, I got sucked into something.

Sorry, I got sucked into something, she texts. *I got sucked into something and I lost track of time.*

She's always getting sucked into things.

Sometimes the men respond, sometimes they're hurt and they never text again. If she hears from them that night, she texts her address. She feels better about casually inviting them over at the end of the night instead of during the day.

Alice likes redheads with messy hair. She likes sex through the underwear, around the underwear, but it rarely happens. She smokes the Tinder men's weed and observes their many-splendored eyebrows.

Tonight the Tinder man isn't responding.

It's late. Alice can smell that something organic has gone off. She wonders if the smell is coming from her. She wonders if she's been smelling this bad all day and then wonders if she's rotting and soon she'll be dead like her brother, but then she sees the halved grapefruit rotting in the nearby garbage can.

Alice always thinks she should bring up her dead brother earlier in conversation because all the best moments in life have real tension. She could say her brother died and she is destroyed, and how can this person standing in front of her ever make any kind of difference to her? Her brother died. Her faith is warped and mangled.

The moon is wading in the black night sky, she thinks. Wading in the kiddie pool sky.
Her brother died and all she could offer was the opposite of proof. A covered up hole in the ground. A name on a stone. A story that somebody once said out loud.

The Tinder man shows up at midnight. He doesn't mention how she flaked on the first set of plans. Alice is wearing a sweater with no bra.

I want your body, he says as his Burberry coat slips to the floor.

The Burberries taste like Burberries, she thinks.

A woman said that to me at the gym the other day, she lied.

She's already very high. She says, *Do you really want this body? Do you want to wear me like a bear skin rug?*

The Tinder man ignores her and reaches for the joint between her lips. Later they burn a pizza together and toss pornographic playing cards across the room, trying to get them stuck in the grates of her tiny space heater.

***

Alice leans back hard into the last church pew. She wants to snap it in two. The wedding ceremony has been dragging on forever. The groomsmen are wearing pastel bowties and the whole thing feels kind of divorcey.

Alice has always believed that weddings are places of conflict. Her parents met at a wedding. Her parents started her family at a wedding.

Alice would have taken her brother as her plus one but of course he died. She promises that from now on, when people die she's going to start saying they murdered themselves. They murdered themselves with cholesterol foods. They murdered themselves with life.

Alice's brother murdered himself with the pointless thoughts that dripped into hardened stalactites in his brain.

Her friend Pat is her plus one, but not really. During the reception he mostly chats up old ladies next to the buffet. She watches him from the singles table. The special catering candles heat the silver trays all lined up behind him. She watches her friend like he is a fantastic film that will never end.

Outside, the black ocean sky is raining. Alice squints through the cold hotel window. She feels like a person looking back on childhood. The role of events in life change over time, she thinks, and she hugs that thought all the way up to her discounted room on the seventh floor.

***

Two days later Alice returns to work. She remembers that she was promoted just before her brother died and she took a long break. She isn't sure whether or not she'll be expected to be the manager when she gets there.

Every day is exactly the same at McDonald's. Soon they'll all be robots. Well, soon they'll all be at home and robots will do the work. The government has no plan for how to deal with that. The government is not for them. For now, the government is against them.

She's still sitting in her car behind the McDonald's even though her shift ended hours ago. The engine is on. The car dings continually to remind her that she's not buckled in.

The moon is waiting in the ocean black sky. The moon will come when you call it. The moon will be sucked under by the currents.

Alice takes her hand off the wheel and reaches into her hair. She gently pokes around and tells herself she is searching for evidence of her brother's murder.

She thinks about how her brother used to say that the world is a collaboration of symbols that were never meant to add up to a meaningful thought. She wonders if he thought that thought on the day he died. She wonders if people have any good thoughts on the day they die.

The emoji for the world is a blue circle with some green splatters on it. She texts three of them in a row to Pat. Pat texts back a yellow thumbs up and a red apple. She takes a blurry picture of herself biting her thumb in her dark car but she doesn't send it. She lets a few drops of blood drip onto her rubber phone case, then rolls her thumb in it. When she pushes the button for the dashboard light, there's no fingerprint, only a smear of pale blood.

***

When she gets home she signs up for a Christian dating website. She lets self-identified Christian men buy her dinner every other night for a month. They spend hours at restaurants named after days of the week. There isn't any sex. After the first few dinners, she starts imagining she's going on auditions to be these men's mother. She hears it in every man's voice. *Are you willing to take care of me?* She knows some of them have weed but none of them offer any.

She takes half of her dinner home in a styrofoam container and eats alone the other nights.

At work she fades into the background, watching as one employee at a time is replaced by an electronic equivalent. The new cashiers are cartoon faces on two foot tall computer screens. Besides pushing the power button, there's nothing else she needs to do to manage them. Pat meets her in back and they smoke the last of his weed. He has also recently been replaced at his job by a car that drives itself.

Pat is staring at a flashing sign advertising the triumphant return of a pork sandwich.

Isn't it nuts that little kids eat food every day even though they don't know why they're doing it? he says. *Or, like, cavemen ate food their whole lives and they had no idea how food works.*

They got hungry, she says. *So they ate.*

But they were just going around and finding stuff they could shove into themselves. That was like the whole point of being alive back then.

Before they unplugged him, machines performed all the normal human functions for her brother. Different sized tubes ran to his mouth and his wrist, secured with medical adhesive tape. His last meal was humid air and IV fluid.

It sounds lovely, she says.

***

That night, Alice receives an email informing her that surveillance cameras caught her smoking behind the McDonald's and that she's fired. The email is from the cameras. The surveillance cameras are the ones who fired her.

It was only a matter of time, she thinks as she drops her nametag into the nearby garbage can. One of the thoughts that haunted her brother taps her on the shoulder but she deftly ignores it.

The moon had been growing bigger each night, and now the moon was the whole sky, and you had to hope that a crater was perched over your bedroom window otherwise it would be too bright to sleep.

She'd been the one who picked her brother up from the therapist after his court-mandated appointments. When he told her that the only fix for his brain would be shutting it off, she'd suggested he drive an hour to an isolation tank she'd read about but had never been to. It cost seventy-five dollars to sit in the dark of the isolation tank for one hour, floating in the extra-buoyant liquid. That seemed like fifteen dollars too much to spend on herself. She wishes she'd offered to pay for him, but what difference could that perfect dark really have made?

There were no more jobs to be had. Alice put a thin rubber band around the stack of unopened bills on the kitchen table. The thermostat hovered at uncomfortable temperatures.

She was mad at herself for being jealous of her brother's carefree deadness. He wasn't around to laugh at her or tell her she was being stupid, so she had to keep thinking that same thought over and over.

Eventually all she could think about was that her problems would never end, but of course that isn't true for anyone. Everything ends, but the brain has no use for finality, so it chooses to forget the lessons of dead brothers.

Instead, things were dire for a while, and then Pat borrowed money from his father and lent it to her. In fact, they all borrowed money from each other, all the people around, and they borrowed other things, and everyone knew everyone. Alice borrowed money from her dead brother. She wore his winter hat and borrowed the smell behind his ears. The government borrowed their labor, which they lent for free until they were tired and needed to sleep under the glow of the moon. The moon borrowed the night sky, and during the day they all borrowed the rays of the sun. They borrowed memories of each other and played them in their heads when they were having trouble sleeping at night. Viruses borrowed their health and they slept on their couches with the TV on. The atmosphere borrowed their breath and returned it promptly. Or didn't.

Everyone and everything was so busy borrowing that no one thought to keep track of who owed who, and they forgot what debts were, and they forgot to renew their vehicle registrations, and whenever they felt a certain feeling inside their stomachs, they went out and found pieces of the world to put in their mouths and chew and swallow.

They chewed and swallowed, chewed and swallowed the moon white sky.

LINDA M. CRATE

my doubts and fears

i feel like
war is on the
horizon,
and my heart weeps;
for i do not like
war nor the people whom
it profits—
my sister just turned eighteen,
and they're thinking of
doing a draft;
and all i can think is of her dying
in some foreign land and both my anger
and my tears form in my heart in
equal measures
i have no kind words for this
president, i did not vote for him, i didn't
want this;
i want america to think and to be kind
again—
i don't see the necessity of breaking families
open into a thousand wounds
because no matter who wins the war we all lose
does the greed of rich men know no
bounds? are we all prisoners of a slavery we cannot
end?
i cannot breathe easy with this administration
every day seems to bring with it new damage
it's only been a week,
and i'm terrified none of us will survive him.

DONNA ZEPHRINE
HOMEWARD BOUND

I return from an active duty tour to find that my house is no longer
my home
I open my door to my house and there is another family living in it
They tell me they have been renting it for two months
I cannot find my wife and kids
I do not know where to look
I had a life when I left
I had friends when I left
They do not feel like friends anymore
I have seldom spoken to them in the last four years
I could still knock on their doors
I'd rather not
I have pride
I do not want to have the same questions about things I do not
wish to speak of
I'd rather sleep on the street
I will find a box or standing shelter
I am strong and have survived sleeping in much worse places
I am not homeless, I just do not have a home right now
I am a hobo
Hobo means "homeward bound"
I am homeward bound,
I just do not quite know where that is yet.

ELAINE GINGERY
Six Months, Max

It is hot and bright and harsh outside, the window glaring.

Inside, where you sit in a plush leather chair, the air is cool, stale, sharp on the tongue and aggressively recycled. He sits across from you, a large plank of oak divides the space between patient and doctor. His face is kind, flat, unpassable while he gives the news, a diagnosis that will have you dead by New Years. You know he's rendered this verdict for others more times than imaginable, sitting in that chair, straining to make you understand the impossible; something that cannot ever really be understood. You know you should ask questions. You should speak. But you can't. That seems to be expected. Your body is tingling, buzzing with information it cannot process, limbs heavy as though they belong to someone else. The roundness of your hips against the leather feels excessive as the curve of your ass shifts in the chair. All the excessive parts of you will melt away, your body like a skeleton before you die. You have seen this before. The hunger fading, the body shifting into something else, the sleep enfolding every hour, the piles of drugs to take, the appointments to keep, the hope that isn't hopeful.

You wonder if you should thank him before you go.

It takes a mere moment for you to know, when you inevitably run into someone, if they already know or not. If they know, they do one of two things: panic at the sight of you, at the evidence of it on your face, their face dissolving in horror, quick and quiet, and then recover enough to make small talk; or their eyes go soft and pitiful and their voices drop into comforting tones, cliches rolling off the tongue as though they are standing in the Hallmark aisle at the drugstore, reading condolence cards, all in a row.

If they don't know, you catch them scanning your body, noticing the weight loss, lingering on the the dark circles under your dull eyes. You consider making them squirm with unknowing, letting them wonder what has taken hold, or telling them outright so they can choose to panic or console.

It's hard to decide which is worse.

Summer drags on. Your body slowly starts to fail. When fall arrives, so do the nightmares. You want nothing more than sleep and yet, sleep is now unsafe. Leaving the house becomes unbearable. People and their hope and their prayers. You stay inside and watch the sun track across the wall, lower now in the sky than Diagnosis Day. Staying home is unbearable, too.

There is endless talk of pumpkin spice everything and yet, everything tastes the same: metallic, gritty, useless, grey. Everyone wants you to eat something, brings you casseroles dishes and pastries. You break off a chunk of muffin and put it on your tongue, trying to smile and "ummmm" while you try not to choke, grasping for water and wondering how much will stay down. They won't leave until you perform this ritual, so you do it, even when it makes you want to tape up the doors and windows and put a hazmat symbol on the front door.

Everyone is so well intentioned but nobody knows what to say.

The doorbell rings and nobody but you is home to hear it. You open the door to a delivery man, package under his arms, young and strong and with a bright, open smile on his face. You wait a moment for his smile to falter, for panic or pity to take over his features.

It doesn't.

Instead, he looks straight at you and makes easy conversation.

"I'm sick," you say, gesturing vaguely at your body.

"Obviously," he replies, without a change in tone. He shows you where to sign but you can't move for gratefulness. Your body feels flooded, full and heavy. Your eyes start to tear up and you don't know what comes next. He smiles and puts the package down on the hallway table, setting his tiny computer on top, his movements slow and deliberate. His eyes are kind and simple and openly looking into yous. "There's nothing to do, right now," he tells you. "Let's just stand here for a moment. Can you do that?"

You nod and start to cry in earnest. He's watching your face, that smile unfailing, and yet, it doesn't feel at all misplaced. You step forward and he easily folds you into his arms, holding up your diminished weight and stroking what's left of your hair.

"I know," he says quietly. You believe him.

The moment stretches out. You can feel your heart, light and fluttery, trying to keep time with the rhythm of his own, strong and insistent in his chest. His breath is subtle, light and regular, while yours drags in and out in ragged moans. You can feel his hands, one at the small of your back, lifting slightly, while the other one works it's way through the motions of comfort. He smells like peppermint and sweat, his uniform scratchy and comforting against your cheek. You're not sure if your feet are on the ground. You're not sure you even have feet anymore. You sink into his body, your heart and breath syncing up with his, easier than they have been in months. He waits while you fall apart and then slowly stitch yourself back together. He waits and doesn't shift his feet or make any more sounds. He is solid and strong and you don't even know his name.

You don't want to know his name.

When your feet come back and can hold you solidly on the earth again, his grip relaxes. You stand up straight and he's still smiling.

"Better, for now?" He asks.

You nod.

He picks up the tiny computer and shows you where to sign, your quivering finger as the pen.

"Last name?" He asks, typing it in quickly as you speak it.

"Thank you," you manage, in a voice that doesn't sound like your own.

"You're welcome," he replies as he walks back out your door.

The nightmares stop.

Three weeks later, the hospice people come.

The light is low and soft on the wall.

No more packages arrive.

STEVE TAGUE
The Farm

1

I try to remember, but I was too young. Too young to remember anything but flashes of things that could be memories, but as the years wear on you, I wonder if they were just dreams. There was so much going on during the years of the Nitro Wars, it's hard to really pin anything down. Of course, there is what The Master tells me. The Master's first rule is: don't question The Master.

He tells me I look good for my age, and constantly apologizes for not keeping better track of time. Things like learning how to not die kind of got in the way. It was a crazy time, I know that.

Now all I know how to do is tend to the Cattle and not die. Well, that's not all I know how to do, but for the most part, that is all there is to do. Up in the morning, wake the Cattle, feed the Cattle, bleed the Cattle. My sole job is to keep them alive, and theirs is to keep us alive so I see the benefits of working together. I just can't help but think that somehow there's more.

The Wolves came last night. Two of 'em. I swear, they know now. I do what I can, but I run this place by myself and the bastards know when I'm getting even the slightest bit of shuteye. They got hold of a Calf and were tearing into it when I got there. Shot 'em both dead and spit on 'em for good luck. Spent the rest of the night nursing the Calf, but there was just too much blood and I had to put her down. I know I ain't supposed to get attached, but losing this one hurt real bad. Something about the look in her eyes just stabs me in the heart.

Things were different before the wars. I lived in a house, I know that. I had a Mom and a Dad, I know that, although they live to me now only in a cloud. After they died, The Master took me in and I was lucky that he spared me. Nobody at that time was getting spared, that's for sure, but for some reason I guess he feels like he needs me. Not just to tend the herd, mind you, but for some other purpose he won't tell me. He remembers the Old World and talks of it constantly, partly as a way to teach me, and partly as a way to maybe keep a world that's long dead, alive in his own mind. I don't know, perhaps it gives him a glimmer of hope.

He only comes out in the night, like all Vampires do, I suppose. There's very little downtime but when there is he talks about the way things used to be. Before the wars. "We didn't know how good it was," he says, "People had jobs and shit, families and shit, you could go out, eat, drink, throw a Frisbee, go to an opera, sit on the beach and do nothing, we had it all man and we fucked it all up. Know why? Me neither, except to say that it's probably been in our nature from the start."

I get some of what he says, I just have doubts about to what degree to believe him. There is one thing I do believe in though, and that is that The Master has kept the Farm going for a long damn time.

When Nitro hit the streets—that was when everything went haywire. It was blood and chaos, the likes of which—well, even that lives in the cloud. I know what I remember and I know what I'm told, but what I don't know is never the twain shall meet. So, hordes of Wolves running wild in the streets tearing people apart may only be a distant memory to me, or it may be a dream, but either way I know it just the same.

The Master is tough on me but it's for a reason, I think. If he wasn't, we would all be dead. He remembers the old days and he might be the last person who does. He calls me BobbyMitchum and when I ask him what that means, he says I wouldn't understand, but that I kinda look like him. Don't know what my name was before, so for now I guess my name is BobbyMitchum.

2

He's a good kid, that Bobby Mitchum. I've taught him well. He's smart, if not exactly bright. I beat myself up every day about the things I haven't told him yet. I imagine I'll need to tell him someday, but I still am coping with the horror of it all myself. Once you've seen a horde of Wolves devour a human being to satisfy their insatiable hunger, it's just never the same. I remember a world where that never happened, but that world is no more.

I need him, though. I need him to keep his head on straight and stay focused. We're far enough out in the middle of nowhere to maintain our current existence, but who knows how long that will last? Wolves come sporadically now, but it's only a matter of time before we get discovered by a roving pack. That will surely be the end of us. I can't have him being distracted from tending to the Cattle, or tending to me for that matter. Thoughts of what once was the world will only eat away at him as they do me, and that would surely jeopardize our safety.

He knows some things. He was 9 or 10 when I saved him from the Wolves that ate his parents. The mind will wash away many things for the sake of maintaining its sanity but certainly not everything. I've taught him the life of the farm I grew up on, and some of the intricacies of the science I made my career out of, back when that was a thing. He asks many questions—but how to tell him?

I'll tell him eventually, it may just be impossible for him to grasp. I owe him that much. For now the Cattle must be fed, the Cattle must be bled. The Farm has to keep running. Our lives depend on it.

3

The Cattle been acting kinda antsy lately. Be nice to have some dogs around, but I guess all the dogs are dead. I think I had a dog once.

I take them out into the field and let 'em wander around. It must be nice to live in that kind of oblivion. To have no knowledge of anything except what's right in front of you. The younger ones are easy. They've been bred into the farm life. We have some older ones that get a little surly sometimes. They're Rescues from the war days and lord knows what they've been through, so they're a bit more unpredictable, but they're old.

I don't bother to bleed the elders anymore, they're just here to eat food and take up space. I still respect them though, because I was taught respect.

Feed 'em, bleed 'em, and breed 'em. That's what I do. Sleep with one eye open. Get up before the sunrise. All the wild animals are gone except for the Wolves. And birds. One of the few solaces I have is listening to the birds sing. Then it's back to work.

We grow grains to feed the herd, vegetables so I can eat, and The Master lives off of the blood of the Cattle. It leaves a lot of time to ponder the meaninglessness and necessity of such an existence. Would I want it any other way? Hell yeah, but the options are null and void. Who, given this life, wouldn't want to go back to the way things were? The irony of it all is remembering the old way and people bitching about how screwed up everything was. Given the way it is now, every damn one of them would kill for something we'll never get back.

We have a rotational system for bleeding to make it as painless as possible. Nobody likes it, but The Master needs the blood so we can all stay alive. The herd is big enough now that I don't have to spike any of them more than once a week. You cut into them, get the blood and send them on their way. I would say it's a text-book process, but nobody had time to write a textbook on how this actually works. The Master is the textbook and I know that because we're still here. The Cattle eat in the morning, I eat in the afternoon, The Master feeds at night. All day. Every day. That's the routine.

The herd has grown on me over the years, and despite their condition they still take on personalities of their own. I've tried to name some of them, but The Master won't let me. "Don't name them," he says, "It'll only make you get attached. They're Cattle. Treat them like Cattle." So I give him what he wants because I like being alive, but in my mind I name them anyway because he can't tell me what I can and cannot think.

The sitting. The waiting. It's excruciating.

4

You can get eaten alive by your own thoughts. That can take years. At least the Wolves are quick about it. I'm riddled with guilt, not just about my part in the carnage of the Nitro Wars but also about the depths I've had to sink to in order to survive the aftermath. There is a special place in Hell for me I know. The only thing I have left to hold onto is one glimmer of hope—that Bobby Mitchum isn't the last pure Human alive. He may well be, I just don't know.

I'm feeling hungry, I must feed soon. I hate it. Every day I feed, I'm reminded of why I have to. Every drop of blood tastes like the memories of what we had and wasted. Every feed is a flashback to a time before.

How to explain the hand I had in developing Nitro? The hand I had cut off at the most crucial moment over greed, power, manipulation, war. I had it right in front of me. It was the cure to so many diseases and the prolonger of life. Ponce de Leon should be buying me shots. Nitro was supposed to save us all. It had to be perfect though. Unstable forms of it would do who knows what, and that's exactly what happened.

They synthesized it in all the wrong ways and dropped it into the population, tried to use it as a way to control people and that's when things got out of control. Gangs using it to fight other gangs, corporations slipping it into their products. I heard rumors they were putting it in the water, and I can only assume the military weaponized it on a worldwide scale. It just spread like a plague.

The internet went dark, phone lines went down, radio signals drew static and I assume the mailman got eaten. Communication turned to zero. Everything was on fire, there were riots in the streets as the panic set in, and the Wolves were turned loose on the masses. Nobody knew what to do and there was nowhere to go. It was total chaos. That's when I came to the realization that Humanity would not be coming back from the brink.

When the Government started abusing the Nitro, I spoke up, made noise, tried to do the right thing. I tried to tell them about the savage nature that it could induce. Begged with them, pleaded with them, but they didn't listen.

That's when they jacked me up. I had to disappear because I knew too much about The Program and was now deemed "unreliable." Two guys from the Agency took me away in the middle of the night and locked me in one of their dark sites. Then they shot me up with enough Nitro to turn me into a puddle on the floor. I suppose the plan was to turn me into a Wolf, but they didn't know what they were doing.

See, what Nitro does when abused is it corrodes the cerebral cortex to various degrees, depending of course on the severity of the abuse and the regulation of the dose. The right dosage and timing turns the subject into what we called a Drudge. Soulless, zombie-like workers with no will of their own. They do what they're told without questioning why. They're fucking slaves, but don't have the capacity to understand the boundaries of their own captivity.

A little higher dosage and you get Cattle. They just wander around in their stupefied state, not knowing this from that. Easy to handle. Easy to herd. Easy to control.

When you really jack 'em up with Nitro, that's when you get Wolves. They roam in packs and devour anything with blood in it. It's brutal. The Wolves were created with one specific purpose: to depopulate.

I got away from the Agency, but now I'm jacked up. I'm what is known as a Vampire. I need the Nitro that's in the blood of the Cattle and it must be done right. One wrong turn and I'll turn Wolf, and then that last light of hope dies along with the rest of us.

Jump ahead to Two Thousand Whatever It Is, and this is where it's at. I have a date with the powers that be, and I'm certain I have sins to atone for. To live off of the blood of your Cattle is one thing, but to know while you're taking them in that there may have been a Somebody in there at any point...I suppose there's a certain amount of Karma that goes into being eaten away by the very thing you feed off of.

Bobby Mitchum is the future. The only one I know of that didn't get with The Program. I believe there are others. There has to be, but I just don't know.

5

The way The Master tells it, the Cattle used to be people, but now there's nothing left of their minds to make them Human. Same with the Wolves, but a pack of Wolves is terrifying in its lust for slaughter and bloodshed. Cattle can be domesticated. Wolves are just blind mayhem whose only purpose is to devour. They howl orgasmically when they really get going and sometimes tear into each other as the smell of the blood drives them into an even greater frenzy.

They can't be brought back either. Nobody can. Once you were turned by the Nitro you were checked out, brother. No more cakewalks, no more movies, no more birthday parties. You just Are Not. The Rescues have a different look to them though, almost like they sort of remember a life that they once had that they are still reaching out to but can't quite get hold of. Kinda like me. There's a look in their eye that says, "I used to be Somebody. Who was that?"

I keep thinking about the Calf I had to put down this morning. Would she have gone to school? Would she have had birthday parties? Would she have gotten her ears pierced and messed around with make up in a normal world? I suppose the possibilities are enough to drive you mad, if you let it.

The sun is going down. Time to bleed.

NOLAN HUTTON

FISH HOOKS HUNG

The urgent care doctor, a veteran of thirty years, guessed
correctly that a coffee table had split my one year old's
eyebrow open. He manipulated the wound
as though he were opening the mouth of a small
fish. Stitch job for sure. After the anesthetic had taken
effect, our son was restrained on a papoose board, and the doctor
had inserted ear plugs, he began to sew his eyebrow back
together with a needle like a fish
hook. Some living things can't recognize a trap. My son fought,
loosening the straps of the papoose board, but could
not escape the nurse holding his head, his father holding
his arms, and his mother holding his legs as the doctor pierced
his skin, drawing the line taut to
cinch the laceration. After the last knot was tied, my son
was carried outside shrieking. His mom pointed at the sky
and said, look at the birds. He chuckled perceptively

because he knew   because dozens of murky
the meaning of the word   stars eddied in
birds and found recognition   the placid sky
                         delightful
on that summer evening   like baited lines
         hung from God   knows where.

SINGLE MOTHER TRYING TO USE THE BATHROOM

The oven timer beeps *Mom*
your daughter says from the other side
of the bathroom door the phone
rings in the kitchen an ominous
thunk resounds from your son's
room Mom your daughter tries the locked
bathroom door phone ringing odor
of burn you listen for movement from
your son Mommy ringing. There is a crack
in the bathroom tile like the inverse of a lightning
strike. The smoke alarm yelps shrilly Mommy
your son yells a muffled stranger's voice like
a JC Penny suit leaves a message you catch
the word balance. Tracing the lightning
with your finger, delicately following its crude
energy into the grout, a hidden plane, silent
            and gaping for 360 degrees.

                              stillness
In this

        the smoke alarm persists.
You flush, then rise, passing through the ceiling
as your home shrinks into the
vagueness of the neighborhood's
dusk, ascending into an exploding
cumulonimbus, innumerable ions
scattered antagonistically
charged, and as only you can,
you gather them in a surge of electric
clarity, pouring plasma down
through the jagged fracture,
mending another broken sky.

Last 4th of July

What I first saw did not appear to be skin,
but a wrinkled felt-like material
as though a puppet was working
its way through the birth canal toward
the surgical lamps framing the doctors head. A mimicry
of life had gestated as I prepared
to become a father. The nine
months had been a bluff. I would not carry
a boy's ego, fragile as a light
bulb, home. Then, in an interval of
Planck's time, he was
bawling as a nurse laid his stout,
disoriented body on his
mother's chest. As close to his home
as he could get, he eyed the room
skeptically. None of us heard the fireworks
outside the Oakland hospital. The country
shrank to the size of that delivery
room. Its history compressed
into the light it took to cut out the
shadow of a mother handing
a son to his father.

GERARDO DE JESUS GURROLA JR.

GIBBOUS

Finalist for the 2017 So Say We All Literary Prize in Fiction

Recovery had not been easy, and not that I ever thought it would, but the bus did not help.

Christmas of last year, I went to La Tienda with my Mom and little brother. It was already evening, and we were buying maza and cornhusks for the tamales we would have helped my grand-ma make. I don't like washing the cornhusks. I always wash the cornhusks.

I was not feeling much of anything. It was not a peculiar night, and there wasn't too much on my mind. My little brother tripped over his left ankle, and caught himself on my shoulder. I didn't remem-ber him being so tall.

The bus is not crowded this afternoon, and I notice a small string that is caught in the worn velvet of the seat beside me. Not velvet, it's scratchy, like a lint brush, but softer. My parents had a lint brush in almost the same color when I was younger. They kept it in the bathroom drawer. I held the lint brush whenever I used the toilet. I thought it kept me from being flushed down.

I admired the string's persistence.

Today I am sitting in the back of the bus beside an open window. The window opens just a little bit, enough to let the air in, but not enough to let us out. My seat faces out the side of the bus, not the front.

I used to get dizzy in these seats before my medicine. I would get too disoriented, the scenery passed too quickly, and the bus vibrat-ed too violently. Now, it seems like front facing seats are deceptive.

I don't move in one direction like I once thought I did; I simultaneously move forward and across. Left to right, but moving ahead. This is the only seat that makes any sense anymore.

It is not just the medicine that makes me think this way. I know I am more than just the Medicine.

I didn't know that Daniel and his dad shared the same name, too. Like me and my Dad. I also didn't know his Dad hated him, too. Like me and my Dad.

I wonder what it would be like if we were actually our Dads. I wonder what our Dads would think. My Mom knew that it was hard for me to be around people, around lots of them. I think she thought I'd grow out of it, but this was not the case. For me, it was something I grew into. I don't know why. I don't suspect I ever will.

We walked into La Tienda, and the door opened to millions of stout women dressed in violent beige. They all seemed beige. It all seemed violent. They chattered, too. As they walked and rolled carts of clinky glass mole jars and crunchy tortilla chips, a throaty tinging floated stagnantly above them.

I became aware of the weight of my tongue in my mouth.

Daniel and I were both drunk, and he had beat me again in Mortal Kombat. I had brought two bottles of wine, and his parents were out for the weekend.

He asked me if I felt bad for losing. I told him I was drunk. He laughed, sinking deeper into the sofa. I leaned my head on his shoulder. He told me Evelyn was not getting back with him, I said fuck her, he said fuck you, I said sure. He said that's why I love you, I told him to prove it, so he kissed me. It was not romantic.

I am still admiring the string. When the sun comes through the window, the shadow cast by it makes it look like a caterpillar. Then it's a string again. Then it's a caterpillar.

The bus stops at caterpillar. The front doors of the bus open to a man with a long, thin, silver ponytail. He walks up toward one of the front seats with a large, gapped smile. He sits next to a woman with a tight bun and sunglasses.

"Hey, you wouldn't know it, would you? Man, you wouldn't even look at the fuckin'
thing--" He trails off and she picks up her bag to move to another seat.

I think I can taste him. His oiled face seems to cast around a mist, and every time he moves, his pony tail swings a bit more of himself into the air. He tastes like something fleshy, something rotten. He is not so much man as he is tongue. If you could imagine a tongue having been cut out of someone's mouth, left out in the sun, and then rehydrated within a bath of mayonnaise, he is probably what you might expect to see.

He looks towards me but I look down. I squeeze the tip of my tongue against my right molars.

I floated past the produce and the seafood, with each step further-ing the distance between my neck and the body beneath it. I used to call it "feeling stretchy" when I was smaller.

It happened a lot playing baseball. My head would wander off when I got into the outfield, and I just wouldn't remember. The game went dark as soon as it was over. So I tried, one time, to stay.

I stood with my cleats planted right next to each other. I dug them into the grass as far as I could. I stared at them, and I waited. As soon as I felt my head rolling off, I stared down and looked at them harder. At first it was slight, almost impossible to notice, but the longer I was there, the further my feet grew away from my face. I saw the outfield, and then the bases. The players started looking smaller, and I could see them moving around the field close to my feet, but I kept going. I could see the cooler that held our oranges and Capri Suns, our parents in the stands, the trees planted along the fences, and the cars parked in the parking lot. I could have stayed up there for hours.

I had to sit on a towel on our way back home from the game because I had peed myself in the outfield. Daniel and I went to the same school, and we sat in the corner of our Spanish class drawing pentagrams and upside down crosses on each other's notes. I didn't think I loved him. I probably did.

He was not very handsome; he was thin and had very long fingers. His feet pointed inside when he walked, and his nose bent at one angle while his jaw bent at another. His teeth appeared to be straight, but the longer you looked, the more you could notice they were just folded against one another.

And still, my favorite nights were the ones that I got to spend tracing the tip of my nose along his crooked jaw, and tasting his tongue between my teeth. Sometimes after, we'd drink some of his Dad's beer and stand in the kitchen, waiting to see if the Earth would really devour Us.

He is turned back to face a couple sitting in the seats behind him, his grin shifting along the alphabet to continue his preaching.

"Those men 'n shirts, who for?! Right?! Touching around like they can!"

I close my eyes and push my face into the leather of my bag. I am thinking of Dr. Ren, her hands on her stomach, demonstrating a breath. She inhales, and her stomach grows into an immaculate womb. She exhales, and it falls back in.

"This will get you in control, your brain will follow your body this time, and not the other way around."

I thought about God, too, and wondered how he could forget to teach me how to breathe. I haven't forgiven him yet.

"But I'm not going to let them! Oh, nah – this is not what my country is," he continues.

A small puddle of spit and sweat gather on the surface of my bag under my nose. I sit back up and breathe with my eyes shut. Pushing my stomach out, I breathe in, and sucking it back in, I breathe out. Again. Again. Again.

I was at the butcher department. We didn't even need meat.

I kept myself close, though, just far enough to keep from the buzzing women. I went along with my Mom and brother, picking some steaks. I stood in front of the plastic wrapped pieces. In one of the clear wrappings was a grey colored skin with white spots. I looked closer to read the printed label. The white spots appeared more porous the closer I got, and the flesh more raw and rancid. The spots began to move. They looked more like long, white hairs, and danced against the greying skin. "Beef Lips".

I could feel my blood rush down into the soles of my feet, and at the same time rush up into my eyebrows. I thought about running through the beige, all those women, back into our car.

But, I could not move. The blood in my shoes stuck me to the floor, and my head floated above the meat. My Mom and brother had already gone to get the husks, and I was still standing there.

I tried to call them for help.

Instead, I stood in front of the beef lips and cried. A beige came over to help me, but stopped before stepping into the thin pool of pee around my shoes.

I went to the beach with Daniel a few weeks after. We sat in a life guard tower, resting our feet against the railings. He was staring at something far away, and I twisted the hairs around his right knee between my thumb and index fingers.

I had finished telling him about Dr. Ren and her breath prayers, and I was nervous about what he'd say. I didn't look at him while I spoke.

Then I told him about something I had read once, about a shadow against the Sun. A plow in the middle of a field had cast a long shadow, and for a moment, it stood perfectly in the circle of the setting Sun. It didn't last forever, but it was perfect.

I looked for an answer in the line of his jaw. He turned to watch my hand on his knee, and then laced his into mine. He still said nothing.

The sun had already gone down, and the fading sunshine was all that was left for us. I moved our hands to my mouth and kissed our fingered bouquet. I leaned into him, and we waited there until the only lights left were the fluorescent ones behind us on the street.

I hear him getting closer to me, and his voice fills every empty space. It's a body that squeezes me up against the windows. I keep breathing, and then I open my eyes.

He has not gotten any closer, but instead directs himself to anyone who will listen. His presence is so thick, it feels like he has always been a part of the bus.

I look over to the string, and I watch it continue to turn. Caterpillar, string, caterpillar.

Finally, the bus stops, I grab the string, and walk out onto the sidewalk. The air outside is hot and dry, and my lungs feel like I've been racing. I crouch down beside the bus stop pole, and look up at the sky.

The Sun has already started to set, but it's one of those skies that holds the Moon and the Sun at the same time. I remember when I thought the Moon could only exist at night. I smile and look down at a crack in the sidewalk. I trace it with my finger. I think the bus has helped.

PAUL DOUGLAS MCNEILL II

ARCTIC SOUNDS

I open my eyes and watch the tiny feet do their little dance under the door. I squeeze my eyes shut, open them again, and watch an exact replay. One more time to be sure. I close and open my eyes, and the third performance lets me know all is okay. Every time I open my eyes, a short, private show. Our thin mattress lies directly on the floor and provides the ideal view. The debut performance caused a panic, but now after a few weeks, I've memorized every step of this little dance.

My wife sucks in a loud gulp of air.

"Oi, bebe," she says.

"New one or old one?" I ask.

"The man had a bunch of hands covered in brigadeiro, and he tried to smother me with a bunch of pillows, but then he turned into DNA."

"I just had one where I was in love with our toilet, and I kept thrusting my hands in the tank and my feet in the bowl, and that's how we fucked."

"Sim, amor," she says as she rubs my head.

A minute or an hour passes, and I turn over and see the shadow man shifting his weight on each foot. A few blinks usually make him disappear. I close my eyes, but the shadow man is still there, rocking back and forth. I try to erase him one more time, but he won't go away. I stare as hard as I can at the dark, but shadow man won't stop swaying. I slowly sit up and swing my open hand at fidgety shadow man. I make contact.

"What the fuck?" I kind-of ask.

"Ai, bebe," my wife says. "I'm scared. I think I hear somebody."

I jump from the bed, grab the empty wine bottle by the door, and walk naked into the living room.

"It's like a bunch of knocking and scratching," she says.

I look out the living room window, at the front door. Nothing. Nothing but four feet of snow, strong winds, and a thick sea of white dust, fog, and haze lit by towers of reflected light that stretch up and across a night that never ends. Heavy steam rises and drifts from every roof. Every few seconds, tiny snow tornados are born and die. I can't help but be amazed that the only horror movie set here was actually filmed in New Zealand somewhere.

"Bebe, let's try sleeping with music or something, sim?" my wife kind-of asks.

We go back to bed, and I try to play our Sleepytime Spotify play-list, but the Internet is out—again. Instead, I listen to the constant Arctic racket. I thought the top of Alaska would be eerily quiet, but it's nosier than our ground-floor Brooklyn apartment, our condo in Beijing, or our ocean-view rental in Rio. The Arctic winds howl as they pass under the house, beat against the walls, shake the tinfoil and plastic covering the windows, and force the house to sway on its pillars. The water pumps groan every ten minutes or so, the heating vents clang and click at odd intervals, and snow machines roar at all hours. Freezing dogs howl, and their stiff chains rattle. Gunshots pound the air. A constant sub-polar symphony. The first few nights in the Arctic, you barely sleep, senses piqued. Every sound might be a looming murderer, and you want to get the jump on the bastard before he takes you down. But, you soon realize that you are just in a standoff with the breeze.

A minute or an hour passes, and a new noise joins the Arctic con-cert: the unmistakable sound of the snow crunching and whining under the weight of heavy boots, and then the clanks and thuds of footsteps on our steel stairs. My wife and I sit up at the same time. She grabs her empty wine bottle; I grab mine. I peak out of our bedroom door, while my wife stands behind me with her nails digging into my arm.

"Call the cops," I say.

At night in deep winter in the Arctic, everyone looks like Death, and a black-hooded Grim Reaper is knocking at our window and trying the knob of our front door.

"Cell's not working, bebe," she says.

Door. Window. Door. Window. Fist. Knuckles. Foot. Fingertips.

"Wait, wait. It's ringing. Hello? Hello? Police? Yes? Someone is at the door. Someone is at my door. There is a man at the door. A man is at the door. Ai, bebe, she can't understand me," my wife says as she hands me the phone.

The hooded man keeps knocking and twisting, knocking and twisting, relentlessly.

"Yeah, can you hear me? Yeah? I am at 1539 apartment B. Someone is trying to get into my house."

"Who is it?" the dispatcher asks.

"I have no idea. Please send somebody."

"What does he look like?"

"He's completely covered. He's got a hood on. All black. Just send somebody over."

"What's he doing?"

"He's trying to get in my house."

"Alright. Where you at?"

"1539 B, next to the Search and Rescue building."

"Alright. We'll send somebody," says the dispatcher.

"Do you want—"

"Sir, they're coming, " she says before hanging up.

A minute or an hour passes, and I just stand in the bedroom doorway, naked, with nothing but an old wine bottle in my hand, hanging, ready to throw or strike. Hooded man keeps up his compulsive
knocking, twisting, knocking, twisting. He looks well-rehearsed at
this little upper-body-only choreography. I stand in the bedroom
doorway, trying to make sure he can't see me. The sodium vapor
lights ooze through the blinds, slashing rows into the darkness
across my face and my gut and our collection of city maps covering
the walls. I briefly think about James and Humphrey and Edward
and Fred and Burt. I look at my Indiana Jones fedora on the hat
rack. I realize the only things standing between hooded man and
me are an empty wine bottle, a flimsy window, cheap blinds that
won't close, and a plastic Christmas tree.

Finally, two new light towers stretch across the haze. I walk over
to the window. A police SUV pulls up. Hooded man turns, sees the
car, walks down our steps, and turns toward the back of our house.
Just before he disappears around the corner, he pauses and everything freezes—as if I had just taken a snapshot. He looks through
our window, the ember of his cigarette barely revealing his face before it's covered with a cloud of half-smoke, half-water vapor. The
light reflects off his snow goggles and hits my eyes. I blink, and
he's gone. I turn to the police officer, who's looking in our window,
briefly examining a naked, shaking man. He puts his car in reverse
and drives away.

"That's it?" my wife asks.

"Maybe he's going after him," I say.

"But he went the other way."

"Maybe he's trying to fool him."

I put a chair next to the window and sit and wait for the officer to return. A minute or an hour passes, and I wake up in the chair with the wine bottle between my legs. A note on the front door reads: "Gone to get locks."

I sit in the chair and think about Joe and Daniel and Macaulay until screaming and an abused snow machine grabs my attention. I pull the blinds aside just enough to see out. My neighbor and his girlfriend are fighting again.

"You're the fucked one!" she screams.

"Get outta here!" he replies, and turns the accelerator on her snow machine.

I just stand, naked at the window, watching this argument on repeat. The two players replaying their parts over and over. The chorus of "You're the fucked one" and "Get outta here" plays on a loop, accompanied by a solo from the snow machine. "Fucked one. Outta here. Vroom! Fucked one. Outta here. Vroom!"

A minute or an hour passes, and my wife returns with a plastic bag full of chain guards and swing bars.

"Bebe, stop snooping for a second and help me put these on the doors," she says.

"In a minute, bebe. I need to look something up on the town's yard sale page," I say.

"I got the locks already. I'm not buying used locks."

"I'm looking for guns."

My wife laughs hard—like my mother used to laugh when I said, sitting in my highchair, "I can make my own dinner."

"Bebe, you can't buy a gun on Facebook," she says—laughing.

"You can here. Pretty cheap."

She looks over my shoulder as I scroll through photos of rifles, shotguns, handguns, piles of guns, half-empty ammo boxes, some artistically posed and framed, some barely visible in blurry, rapidly snapped shots.

"We aren't buying a gun, bebe," she says.

"Amor," I say. "After last night—"

"Babe," she says as she pets my head and scratches my beard. "We aren't buying a gun just cause you got scared."

She starts drilling holes into the door jam just as the Search and Rescue helicopter lands nearby, and I stare at the Christmas tree lights through the haze of my freshly brewed coffee and try to drown out an orchestra of buzzing, whizzing, grinding, swooshing, screaming.

CRAIG EVENSON
WAITING FOR YOU

elbow in elbow
pushing twin strollers
with your dozens
of different expensive purses
explosive prayers
shoes
don't get me started on tattoos
I can't see
black abaya floating through
the revolving door
shopping bags
bugs in scrubs and suits
and diers hunched and shuffling
canes   walkers
languages and luggage on wheels
U.S. Minnesota and Mayo flags
high rolling
the way you all swing your arms
or don't especially
if you're holding a paper cup
or a phone
or flowers
and there's one without

one foot past the other
into the future
where it all might happen
only the watcher is present
where it does

thinking nicely
that what you are thinking

can never be as important to you
as my sitting here
looking at it
through the window
of the Kahler Motel might be
to where we are both together going.

POUYA RAZAVI

ECHOES

Finalist for the 2017 So Say We All Literary Prize in Fiction

The mirror shattered. It was the sixth one this month. Sitar looked at her dozen reflections in the fragments. Her face concealed with drops of blood, she looked away. Dragging her fingers across the carpet beneath her bed, she felt the snag of another cut. Bloody hands and light-headedness aside, Sitar was in a buoyant mood. She gathered the broken pieces. Put away the hair straightener and made her way to the bathroom. Leaning on the ridged wallpaper of the corridor, she left bloody marks.

The phone rang as she rinsed and tried to remember where she might have put some plasters. On the third ring, she grabbed a towel and wrapped it around her knuckles. Egyptian cotton pulled tight as a ward against the throbbing. The sting of the cut and her wooziness would have to wait.

"Hello?" She answered the phone and relaxed into the sofa.

"Hi, is this Ms. Wainwright? It's about your mother."

The ominous tone told her it wasn't an earnest provider of legal remedies on mis-sold insurance. Or someone chasing a lapsed standing order for a charity. Sitar didn't want to ask the follow-up. She waited, letting the pause fill the gap, staunching her blood with the towel.

"I'm afraid she's had a bit of an accident. She's hurt herself again."

It was the sixth time this month. The woman on the line didn't need to tell her. Memory, sense and coordination all lapsing.

"We need to discuss what the best course of action for your mother might be. I'm afraid, as you know, we're not equipped for this sort of care. We're a pastoral environment for able-bodied senior artists."

The transition point had arrived for her mother. They had talked about it before and they would need to have the conversation again. There was no point putting it off any longer. Sitar arranged to come in later that week.

Hanging up the phone, she gripped the towel, lay back and closed her eyes for a moment. Drumming her fingers on the sofa's arm, she hovered between consternation and dozing off.

The waiting lasted five minutes or so. The door knocked. She got up, taking the letters and parcels off the postman. Closing the door, she thought of her mother, Dolly. Not as she was now but back in the house in Granger. She became a child when she pictured herself there. Moss-covered stone walls dripping with vines, her playing in the uncut grass. They had lived there in that brief wondrous period of her mother's commercial success. It was Sitar and Dolly only plus her mother's feverish work. Pieces of which now hung in galleries from New York to London.

Even at her best, Dolly was a bit potty. Eccentric, they called her whilst in her prime. The fresh paint on canvas dried up and there were long sojourns into destructiveness. Only then did she pick up the label of madness. Once inspired by a few joints in the early morning, she then disappeared into bottles of wine at night. Dolly's wild curly red hair became frazzled and dying, her rose-bulb face bloated and bruised.

The men came and went like tornados turning Sitar's home upside down with their passing. Leaving behind wailing and overwrought desolation. Then binge sessions that would last until Dolly's hospitalisation for some drunken mishap.

After the sixth such incident, twelve-year-old Sitar replaced the glassware with plastic. Sold all the mirrors in the house. Every time her mother returned the fresh promises would shatter into new fragments.

Dolly sold the Granger house and Sitar went to live with her aunt, Eileen. The last years of school in safe and dull suburban north London. Dolly didn't write or visit, her aunt wouldn't mention any news and Sitar didn't ask.

***

The vibe was good as they all sat in a circle on the thin dusty carpet cross-legged, listening. Jamar was talking, the sheen on his afro sparkling in the candlelight. Palms flat on the ground, his long fingers stretched out pointing at Dolly.

"You get it? Yeah. You either get it or you don't. They wanna put a label on it. Build a box around it. Make it square. That's how it goes, yeah? Out there." He pointed at the doorway of the spacious unfurnished Georgian room. The walls were covered in bright pinks and sunny yellows, deep blues and spirals of green. White symbols for disarmament and doves spelling out 'Peace.'

"But you can dig it, yeah?" He looked at Dolly and she watched his eyes dart, cleavage to face.

The pow-wow in the derelict mansion went on a bit longer. Thick incense and sweet dope blended with anticipation. As the group drifted into pairs and threes, Dolly took Jamar's hand. They went to a corner of a room littered with mattresses. She didn't say anything and he was too hungry to talk.

Afterwards, as he lay sated, she found her pad and charcoal. She sketched his sleeping lithe body. When the sun rose, he woke to see her smoking by the window.

"This is something," he said picking up the sketch, "beautiful."

She turned to look at him.

"You are beautiful," he said.

With a sharp laugh and wave of her hand, she went back to smoking. Gathering his white loose-fit shirt and slipping on his jeans, he got up. There was a brief hesitation, looming over her, bending a little, lips gathered. A ring of exhaled smoke and he turned away, saying nothing. The paper curling on their bedspread remained. Thick etches like an ebony statue, the shade and spaces of a resting lion. Dolly didn't bear look at it.

Checking herself in a hand mirror, she fixed her lipstick. Then leaning out the window, she dropped the mirror and heard it smash.

Getting up, she packaged the pad and charcoal, hiding it under a loose floorboard. She joined others in the damp cold room downstairs. The candles were out and the sunlight hooded by clouds. The room bleached of the possibilities of the previous night.

"Come on," she said to the few huddled together in a listless hangover, "let's go into town and get some breakfast. I'm buying."

They left those sleeping to hold "squatters' rights" and walked down the gravel path. Jumping the gate with its warnings against trespassers. The street of large faux Tudor houses ran westwards. They went into a long road of towering concrete labyrinths and parsimonious cottages. Then they were in a messy high street of shops, stalls and discarded cardboard. It bustled with shoppers and hawkers. Diving into a tight side-lane, they saw Kathy's Cafe. The yellow-painted-frame and tilted blinds, bells jingled as they opened the door. Working men, cramped into plastic chairs, flared their nostrils as the wind hit them. After a look, they returned to their cups of milky tea.

The six of them crowded on two adjacent tables and waited for the girl with the Farrah haircut to make her way over. Breakfasts complicated by vegetarian demands ordered, they waited. Instant coffees and weak tea arrived. Dolly put a tenner on the table.

"Another one sold?" asked Mike, the boy with the thin moustache and tennis player's headband.

Dolly was the only one making any money and she didn't mind sharing. Oil-on-canvas portraits, rustic scenes and young models, were popular. She had sold four to the middle-class patrons of Mamma's Finest Pizzeria where they hung.

"Tacky rubbish," she said. "But the two-point-four-kids crowd dig it."

Raising his white mug, Mike toasted, "Well, here's to you selling out!"

The table chorused and laughed, warm food and working heaters lifting the spirits. Dolly was coasting in Bradford, she knew it. Same crowd, worn out ideas. Waiting for the jolt, the present boredom too much in balance with fear. Finishing her breakfast, she decided tonight's gathering would be her last.

***

The green by Legrams Lane was quiet. Sitar pulled up her coat collar to protect her from the cold. Nobody else on either side of the road, the overcast sky adding to the gloom. A folder with her mum's important documents in hand, she was keen to get out of Lidget Green. Curtains twitched as she crossed over, side-stepping parked cars. There was a mini-cab office past the dishevelled trade union building, about half a mile down the road. Hopscotching across the cracked pavements, she noticed the windows with BNP posters. Rowdy little bull terriers jumped at the gates as she passed.

Lost in her thoughts, she didn't see him on the other side of the road until he shouted out, "Oi!"

Over the roofs of a hatchback, she saw his shaved lumpy white head. Wearing tattered denim, every inch of his skin bar his face inked. Gothic script and obscene distortions of female beauty. His Doc Martins drummed in an echo of her own skipping.

"Nice t-shirt," she shouted back. She slowed to a leisurely pace. Waited for him to overtake and cross over the road. He stood in front of her, blocking her path. Pointing at his Black Flag t-shirt, she cocked her head and stood her ground, blowing him a kiss. Glaring, his face contorted, reminding Sitar of a pig's snout rooting in the dirt. Laughing, she said, "You big muppet. What ya like?"

Bounding in great big steps towards her, he pulled himself close, his chin lined up to the top of her head. Bending down, he put both arms around her waist and lifted her. Planting kisses on his face as she slid down, Sitar had one heel raised, arms cradling his shoulder blades. Giddy, she bit his lower lip.

"Can't believe you were around and didn't bother to knock," he said.

"It's never a quick visit with you, Jack."

"No," his eyes had a roguish glint, "we got some catching up to do."

"Next time, I promise."

They were leaning on a parked Toyota, his hands bracing her waist. Her fingers probed his back and arms. Drops of rain fell and dripped down his jacket. Their lips interlocked as the downpour intensified.

They couldn't ignore it any longer. They raced down the street hand in hand until they came to the cab office. Within the shelter of the smoke-stained walls, he waited for her to speak.

"I've got to sort out my mum," she said.

"She's worse?"

Squeezing his hand, she broke free. Sitar ordered a cab from the squat man with a cigarillo heavy with ash drooped on his lip.

"Soon, I promise," she said as her fingers pushed back his lips. Pulling her jacket up to cover her hair and the paper folder, she stepped out and into the cab.

**

Wrapping her scarf around the cut on the boy's arm, Dolly watched bottles of piss arc through the sky. Most fell short of the line of beleaguered police. The crowd in front of Dolly was a couple of hundred, held back on the pavement behind the barricades. Tending to the long-haired boy, Dolly listened to the agitations of the mob. The boy dressed in bell-bottoms had a blood-stained floral shirt.

"There's a bigger crowd coming," he said. "Where you from, angel?"

"Bradford," she said as they retreated to the safety of the Post Office.

"What brings a nice Yorkshire lass like you down to New Cross?"

"Union business," she said and they both laughed.

Making a pile of Socialist Worker papers she sat next to the boy. They had exchanged names but she couldn't remember his or hadn't heard it over the noise. It didn't matter now. He reached into his jacket and pulled out a packet of Embassy cigarettes. Taking two, Dolly lit them and passed one back to him. They watched the scrum as chants against the Nazis and the pigs mixed with the sound of shattering glass. Makeshift clubs, gate posts and iron girders, cracked bones. The stomp of feet on Fronters with an audible crunch.

As they dragged the last embers and threw away the stubs, the battle finished. Surviving combatants in jubilant mood sung "We stopped the Front." Some still spitting on the Nazis in the gutters. A militant few gathered in clumps, pressing past the broken police ranks. They headed towards Lewisham High Street. Only the union types, clergy and the worn-out stayed.

"Right," the boy got up to join the others.

There was no point trying to talk him out of it. "Keep that wrapped tight," she told him.

The ones left were indistinguishable to her. Long-haired and dressed much alike, white skin on both sides of the fight. The black men loaded up with dustbin lids and cricket bats had gone on. They had the look of men too long with a boot on their neck; wanting some payback. But the white boy, like the others looking to get into some aggro, was an idealist, a dreamer.

"If not now, when? If not here, where?" they chanted before it all kicked off. They wanted the fight, the heroism of standing up to real goddamned, here-and-now Nazis. More than one claimed his grandfather had done the same. They chided their middle-class parents for their passivity.

Dolly liked them but this wasn't for her either. The carnival of would-be revolution, the hunt for a glorious role in the world. It was another sort of theatre. A pretence the majority would walk away from, sliding into comfortable mortgaged lives.

Tired of the biting cold and damp stack of pamphlets, she got up and followed the trail of the crowd.

***

The minibus dropped Sitar off outside the driveway. Clutching her large black bag in front of her chest, she paused before walking up to the door. The sign above the doorbell declared the house a place of therapeutic support. An artistic community with a Christian ethos. A woman in a green woollen cardigan answered with a genteel smile, "Welcome to Holly House, I'm Angela."

"I've been here before. To visit. My mum is staying here," Sitar explained as she followed.

"Oh, that's lovely. I'm sorry I've not seen you before." Angela didn't mention she'd been working at the house for four years now.

The narrow corridors of the Victorian lodge house led to an annexe of modern bedrooms. At the top of the wooden stairs, Angela knocked on a door with a calligraphed nameplate.

There was no response after the second knock, so Angela used her key to open the door.

"Everything alright, Dolly?"

"Yes, yes, is it dinner time already?"

"No, dear, you have a visitor."

Dolly rinsed a paintbrush in a water pot and looked at the door. Her face didn't change as she studied Sitar, partly shielded by Angela. Recognition came, a broad smile formed on Dolly's face.

"Oh, my love! Sweet little Sitar!"

Angela turned back to Sitar, her face brightened with relief. "I'll leave you two to it."

"Well, are you not going to give your mother a hug?"

"Of course," Sitar embraced her as she remained seated on the stool.

"They put it in your head I'm going batty, didn't they?" Dolly said. "Don't believe everything you hear. They're trying to up the rents again. And I'm not having it!"

Her daughter didn't argue, instead looked at her current work. The canvas was diagonal lines interlaced into a thatched rainbow of colour. The edges an empty white frame. It made Sitar think of a plaster over a seeping wound.

"Do you like it?"

"What happened to Rollo?" The small Yorkshire terrier was no-where in sight.

"Who? Oh, your brother. I'm sure he'll be around soon."

The room was neat. Art supplies in plastic containers and rolls of canvas in tubes, tidy in the corner. Books stacked on a desk and organised by theme on the shelves. Clothes put away in drawers.

"I told you," Dolly said, "I'm not going mad, yet."

Sitar sat on the bed, letting go of the bag for the first time. Hints of rosewater and her mother's perfume threw her back to childhood.

"Cup of tea?" Sitar asked a tremble in her voice.

"Oh, let me. Green ok? The doctor says it's good for me. Besides, I can't stand that soy milk rubbish."

They sipped at their tea, appraising each other. The vagaries of age and eventful lives had left their marks. Both their eyes full of fire, a wilfulness that had passed in the blood.

"I appreciate you not mentioning how long it's been since I visit-ed," Sitar said.

"At your age, I wouldn't get caught dead in a place like this." Dolly went to the tall standing mirror with the crack down its length. She straightened her pale-yellow dress and matted down her grey hair.

"But I should've come sooner."

Dolly took out an old shoe box from under the bed. Parting the lid, she revealed old black and white photos on long faded paper. Pictures of men and women, about Sitar's age. Mixed lives, some dressed up hippies, some dressed down suits. Clouds of smoke, bottles of beer. Urban landscapes that looked weathered, near economic collapse. London and Bradford, in parallel lines.

"All these places have their moments," Dolly sang, tidying the photos back into the box.

LUCY PALMER

THE QUICKENING

A net force produces a change in momentum that is equal to the force multiplied by the time interval during which the force was applied.

You took me for coffee. I spoke for nearly two hours, the words spilling like rain, said the things I'd never been able to say out loud. You listened intently but didn't say a word, just sat with your giant tombstone hands palming your lap, occasionally sipping your cappuccino. You didn't tell me you were sorry for my loss and for that I was grateful.

Because the heart has its own electrical impulse, it can continue to beat when separated from the body.

She is perfect. Skin mottled, eyes squeezed shut as she cuts the air with her first cry, warm and alive and so damned beautiful. You hold her as if she's made of glass, your heft making her seem even smaller, a peanut of a thing. Your heartlove is evident in every ounce of you.

At night, I dream of his small bones, how they grew inside me, how I tried and tried, took the vitamins, ate the right food, but I couldn't keep him alive. I called him Ben—simple, but sweet and strong. Sometimes I feel like he's still inside me; my ghost baby. I feel small kicks as I palm the loosened skin of my stomach.

An inelastic collision is one in which some of the kinetic energy of the colliding bodies is lost. This is because the energy is converted into another type of energy like heat or sound.

It's another time, another place. I tell you how he doesn't touch me anymore, how my flesh disgusts him, though he won't say the

words. My body failed him. Failed us all. As I speak, you place
one of your oversized hands in mine. Then you're kissing me with
those thick lips and all I know, all I feel I've even known, is fire.
Memory dissolves into molecules, for just a moment.

I tell you about that cold October night studded with stars when I
first held him in my hands. How he died inside me the day before
I birthed him—deathed him—and how his skin was luminous,
his feet two tiny cashews, his hands balled into the smallest fists
you've even seen. He was perfect and I could almost believe it
was going to be alright, that if I willed it hard enough he'd take a
breath. But he just lay there, a stone in my palm.

Your eyes tear up as I spoke, and you grip your hands together as if
you're saying a prayer.

*Two moving objects, both possessing momentum by virtue of
their mass and velocity, collide with one another. Within the system created by their collision, there is a total momentum that is
equal to their combined mass and the vector sum of their velocity.*

The first time was in the history section of Adams Avenue book-
shop. I thought I was alone in one the many nooks and crannies
and allowed the tears, allowed myself to remember. I didn't think I
was going to survive.

I didn't hear you approach—I just heard a deep voice asking if I
was okay. Looking around I took in your heft, your solid shoulders,
your kind face with its grey pall that made you look tired; but your
eyes, your eyes were so alive. You smelled of citrus and leather and
salt.

*Every day, your heart creates enough energy to drive a truck for
20 miles.*

And I'll never forget his bones, never not feel that heaviness in
my belly, in my heart. But here you are, burning kisses down the
riverbed of my back, kissing me back into being as she sleeps on in

the bassinet next to our bed. You are here and your fullness, your opacity and her sweet breath, her morning cry, help me remember to take the next breath, and the next.

YVONNE HIGGINS LEACH

We Cancel Thanksgiving Dinner After the 2016 Election Results

The undulating balloons of Mickey Mouse
and Snoopy will graze the sides of buildings
five stories high. Those ropes break
and they will capsize into the crowds below.
Nothing will elevate us above the outcome,
so we cancel Thanksgiving dinner.
With the family on both sides,
the communal table would unravel the imminent:
The first stones to be thrown
over the savory haunch of the Butterball turkey
will be words formed into sentences that accuse,
forks full of mashed potatoes
striking the air. Sentences will form
into paragraphs that make wrong assumptions,
no one listening,
everyone talking,
and defenses shooting up like walls
near the sweet potatoes and green beans.
So much said with hackles high,
the wine becomes distasteful.
Our forks and knives will wave like weapons
with every nasty complaint
that even the candlelight reflecting
in our silverware
won't be able to save the evening.
We will never eat the pumpkin pies.

WALTER, WRONGLY CONVICTED

Incarcerated 28 years

On the flip side of night, he rises
to a mute morning, the hive
of metal and men, moving
in their papery presence,
tethered to another vanishing day.
His daily routine repeats
in a capsule of dwindling time;
the complaints shake in his
muscles and bones, exiled so long
now he can't remember his
before life, the once-way
of family, friends, work, and church.
As a child he watched the daylight
perform a nostalgic dance
in his house. Each day, here, he attaches
to the daylight, even if it is anemic
or leaking away, because even then,
it is the closest he can get
to the hands of God.
The nonjudgmental, unconditional love
of daylight as it watches him eat, work,
eat, work, eat, and read.
And at the end of the day,
he thinks patience is a kind of
insanity, really.
He cups his hand in front of his face
as the fluorescent lights turn off in the coffin
of his inescapable world.
His breath stammers
yet another trembling prayer.

ALEX BOSWORTH

SUMMER OF '76

It was mid-June, 1976. The U.S. was preparing to celebrate its two-hundredth birthday amid the chaotic wake left by Watergate and Vietnam. Whereas I was not quite eleven and was dealing with my own problems, chief among them, having fallen in love with my younger brother's third grade teacher, Helga Guiterez. She was my first and only heart's desire. But how could it ever work? I was a ten year old Caucasian Cub Scout from La Mesa and she was a thirty-year old, second generation, Mexican-American elementary school teacher from the Spring Valley. It was like "West Side Story." I'd stop off at her classroom most every afternoon, under the auspices of walking my brother home. She often complimented me on my haircut or asked how my day had been. She called me *Alejandro*.

On the last day of school, I made her a card with a crude drawing of the two of us, me and her, holding hands. "Be with me, always." it read. But I arrived to find her classroom empty. She'd let her students out early for vacation. I ran out to the parking lot. Her Toyota was gone.

I hung my head, trying not to cry and I saw Mrs. Guiterez's pocketbook lying there. She must have dropped it getting into her car. I took out the drivers license to find her street address.

Helga smiled with surprise at finding me at her front door.

"Alejandro!" she said. "You came here all by yourself?"

"Yes. I found this." I handed her the small leather bag.

"Ah, my purse! I've been looking for it! Thank you! Come on inside, I'll make you some something to drink." I followed her to the kitchen.

She placed the pocketbook on the counter and opened a cupboard. "Do you like Tang?"

I hated it.

"I love it!" I said.

While she was taking a pitcher and an ice tray from the fridge, I pulled the home-made card from my pocket and placed it on the counter. Handing me a glass of cool, orange, astronaut beverage, Mrs. Guiterez noticed the folded piece of purple construction paper. "For me?" As she read the words inside, she put her hand to her chest and sighed. "Ah! You're the sweetest boy I've ever known, Alejandro."

As fate would have it, I had turned to tell her something just when she leaned down to kiss me on the cheek, and our lips met. It was one of those moments in life that arrive without warning, sweeping you up into a world you never want to leave. Sadly, it was over all too soon. At the very moment we'd kissed, the kitchen door swung open and there was her husband, staring at us.

"Steven!" Helga gasped.

"Who this hell is *this*?!" he shouted.

"Don't get excited now, baby!"

"Don't baby *me*! What's he doing here?!"

"He's just a boy who had my purse!"

The man stomped forward, throwing me against the fridge. He grabbed Helga by the arm with one hand and snatched the card away from her with the other. "Be with me, always?!" he growled in disbelief, then turned in my direction, his eyes ablaze with jealousy.

"I love your wife!" I announced, unable to stop the words escaping from my mouth.

"What?!" He let go of his stunned spouse and moved in on *me*.

Helga jumped onto Steve's back, digging her fingernails into his eyes. Enraged, the man pulled her hands from his face and spun around, tossing her onto the dining table. He grabbed her by the neck and began fiercely throttling her. I grabbed a nearby broom and swung it as hard as I could. The wooden handle broke apart as it smacked against the back of his knees. Howling in pain, Steve had stumbled backwards on the brink of falling when Helga took a cast iron skillet from the stove, lifted it on high and brought it down onto Steve's head with a sickening clang.

His body went limp and he collapsed onto the floor, blood gushing from his scalp. Helga was instantly atop his motionless body, one knee digging into his chest, as she repeatedly bashed his skull with the frying pan. Wide-eyed and breathless, I witnessed the mayhem with my back pressed to the refrigerator as if held there by magnetic force.

Finally, she dropped the skillet and collapsed aside her husband's body, attempting to catch her breath. "We have to get out of here!" she said, panting heavily.

"We *what*?!" I gasped. "What?! *We*?!"

"Help me get rid of the body." Helga groaned as she pushed herself up onto her feet. "We'll leave California, maybe the country!"

"I can't! It's Friday! We're having fish sticks! Then I have to take out the trash or I get in trouble."

"Don't you understand, Alejandro!" she hissed, grabbing me by the shoulders. You *are* in trouble! We just killed my husband!"

"But there was a purse! And I took the bus. You kissed me and you made Tang. I hate Tang!"

Helga's hand landed across my face with a loud smack. "Don't fall apart on me now!" she commanded. "I need you!" Helga looked away, as if she could see some place far off in her head. "Listen! It's going to be all right. All we need to do is stick together, just like you wrote. Be with me... always!" Her dark, fathomless eyes met mine as she said, "In the garage, there's a shovel, go get it."

"I don't know if I should—"

"Go get it!" Helga growled, pointing toward the garage. Then she glanced down at the corpse. "There's a hacksaw in there—better bring that, too. I only have kitchen-size garbage bags."

I got the shovel and saw and returned to the kitchen to find Helga going through Steve's wallet. "Damn! There's only six bucks in here! Do you have any cash?"

"Twenty-seven dollars. But that's collection money from my paper route; I'm supposed to turn it in tomorrow."

"Well, that should get us a tank of gas, some food and a motel room for the night, anyway."

"Poor Mr. Guiterez," I said, looking down at the mess on the floor.

"That's not his name! Mr. Guiterez was my second husband."

"Oh. So, this is your third?"

"Fourth. Let's get to work." She took the saw from me and started in on Steve's left leg.

"Can't we just leave him?"

"Are you joking?! His family drops by without warning all the time! If they found him like this, they'd know what happened, and they'd go right to the cops! I've had problems like this before... look, stop asking questions and get a mop!"

Once Helga had sectioned Steve into five pieces, she bagged them up and put them in the trunk of her Corolla while I mopped and sponged the kitchen clean. She took a bottle of tequila from beneath the sink and poured a splash into my Tang before taking a long chug for herself.

I hesitated, then tossed the vile mixture back. It tasted the way I imaged bug spray would and burned as if I'd drank from a lava lamp. But, after reflecting on what I'd just seen and the possibilities of what lay before me, I slammed my hand down and held out the glass, requesting more. The second shot was nastier than the first. "Aagghh!" I choked. "There was something else in there!"

"Aye," she said, studying the bottle. "You swallowed the worm."

After sunset, we drove out east and disposed of the body deep in a wooded area. By then, Helga had polished off the rest of the Mescal and was in no shape to drive. So, with some basic instructions, I got behind the wheel and we headed toward the border.

We spent the next six weeks in Mexicali, living in what passed for a motel. Helga got a hold of some fake Omega watches for me to sell on the street, while she danced at a club and pick-pocketed here and there. We managed to keep a moldy roof over our heads and ate food with some kind of meat in it three times a week. Late at night, we spooned in tattered bedding, whispering sweet nothings to each other, if only to drown out the noise of distant sirens and vermin battling it out within the walls.

Then came that day when I walked in to find our room abandoned, with nothing left behind but the card I'd made for Helga. I burned it after reading it, because she'd written where she planned to go underneath my loving words and I didn't want anyone to find her. I collect called my parents who contacted the authorities who brought me home.

I refused to answer any questions about Helga. The police said I'd go to jail if I didn't talk. My parents tried to loosen my tongue as well, even threatening to cut off my allowance indefinitely. But I was a stone on the subject. The only time I spoke of her was when the police psychologist showed me an anatomically correct doll and asked me where Helga had touched me. My answer was to reach out and put a finger to the place on the doll where a heart would be.

"There." I said. "She touched me there."

JED WYMAN
SPARKS

Hazel wasn't sure what he thought of the band anymore, or Pauly, or working in the greasy spoon in the back of Harley's Bar. The newness he'd once attached to living in Missoula had given way to scuffed familiarity. A soft mist had been replaced by a world cut and dry and paper thin. He eyed the Stratocaster leaning in the corner, its missing strings hinting at a greater incompleteness. He heard the needle spinning on the inner groove of the record and wondered if he had time for one more song before work, and if so, what might it be?

When he got to Harley's, the place was quiet. That was when he learned that Mulrooney had died and the neon signs took on a somber glow. The bar struck him as dustier than usual, his pre-shift drink watered down. Mulrooney's barstool was empty and it felt, to Hazel, that if he were to approach it he might suddenly find himself in some strange bar where the bartender didn't know his name and never took his order. That empty stool was testament to change, to the ultimate disconnect. Hazel stood for a moment, his pack partially unslung, drink in hand.

Madrone "Makers Mark" Mulrooney had lived an eventful life, the last ten years of which he'd spent sitting at the bar in Harley's telling anyone who would listen about it. The stories were always the same, but there were a lot of them, and they never got stale. Not the way Makers told them—his older brother sneaking him in to see Buddy Holly, packing mules in Montana; his two stints in the service, five years apart, the first in the army, the second in the navy. When asked why he'd re-enlisted he'd say, "I didn't know I had until I woke up on the train to boot camp. 'Oh no,' I said, 'Here we go again.'" He'd roadied for The Byrds and, later, The Eagles, where he'd been drinking buddies with Joe Walsh. Friday nights when the bluegrass band would set up in the corner, Mulrooney, announcing that he was feeling "vibrantly sensationalized," was a whirling dervish, dancing with all the ladies and copping feels.

The necklaces Makers wore would swing about, wrapping themselves around the neck of the pint bottle he carried in his breast pocket, which the bartenders allowed. They'd seen him with the shakes. He'd kept a collection of denuded feathers in his hatband making him look like a Robin Hood who had just been rolled. These flew out at intervals, joining the fray that was his wake. After each dance he would stand, breathing heavily, a tangled mess, a jalopy about to overheat, a grin on his face. "Hell," he would bellow, "I haven't had this much fun since I went A.W.O.L. in Managua!"

***

Hazel put on an apron and walked into the kitchen. The sinks were going, the suds rising like gathering cumulus. Betsy, his boss, watched him come in. "You heard the news?" she asked.

"I heard it. How did he go?"

"It's what you'd expect. His liver quit on him, then he got pneumonia." Tears welled up in her eyes. "I don't know if I can work today," she sighed. "The place just isn't the same without Makers. I mean, no one has patted my fanny this morning." She flung a hot pot into the sink. "I'll be back in a minute." She headed toward the alley wiping her eyes.

Makers claimed that being the only Irish-Mexican in a thousand miles made him the man for the job. He claimed to be an ambassador of Bacchus. "I'm ordained, goddamnit, to make sure you all have a goddamn good time, so let's get with it, goddamnit. Let the wine pour freely! Embrace abandon, my pickled pilgrims. Embrace abandon!" he'd say before bursting into "Garry Owen."

If Hazel had known just how little time Makers had left, he probably would have winced at these moments, especially the long uninterrupted pulls on the pint bottle. He chose not to remember *that* Makers, the one who, despite an unflagging lust for life, made Hazel aware of a certain powerlessness in the face of inevitability, rather he would remember the Makers he would find pulling stools off the bar when he showed up for the morning shift at 7:00 a.m. "How's it going, kid?" Makers would bark when Hazel came through the door. Despite the fact that Makers would have a pretty good shake going on, and that he would be halfway through his first drink, which Hazel knew he wanted nothing more than to sit down and deal directly with, Makers would help Hazel set up the place, turning on lights and wheeling out dirty apron hampers. And when Makers asked Hazel how he was, it was real, more real than it was coming from a lot of so-called friends. Now that Makers was gone, Hazel saw just how real it'd been. He wasn't sure why Makers had taken a shine to him.

Betsy came back in after a while. "It's going to rain. Seems appropriate."

"When are they going to have the funeral?" Hazel asked.

"Makers gave his body to science. His organs are going to the research center at MSU."

"Jesus, whoever works with those'll get drunk just from the fumes. They're a contact-high waiting to happen."

Betsy snorted. "Some poor nerdy research student is going to do a face-plant in his brain. There's fifty years of rotgut and brick-weed in there waiting to clobber someone."

"Can't believe it finally caught up with Makers. He was clobbered all the time so I got to thinking of him as clobber-proof."

"I know," Betsy said softly, staring out at his empty barstool. "There'll be a wake here at the bar Sunday. A big party. We figured that's the way he would've wanted it."

"I'm sure he would have. We'll have to play some Buddy Holly."

"And some Joe Walsh."

Hazel got to the sink just before it overflowed.

***

That day was slow, the bar dark, lethargic, the sadness palpable. The ceiling fans whirred.

At the end of the day Pauly and Justine came in. "Hey, Hazel. I got great news! I got us that gig in Bozeman!" Pauly announced. They'd wanted a Bozeman gig for their band, The Erratics, for a long time. "And we're staying at that chick Farrah's house!" He gave a wide-eyed, suggestive nod, "It's Friday night. I've already told Jason and Doug. Doug's going to get a new high-hat. Justine'll help drive down some of the gear."

He could see Pauly's girlfriend, Justine, sitting on a barstool, her elbow propped on the bar, her cheek stretched by the palm supporting it. She took a second to look in his direction and gave a smile. She had been a part of the Missoula rock scene when Hazel arrived in town and possessed a cynicism that Hazel found both sexy and intimidating. A part of her peculiar etching, she drove a '71 GTO.

Hazel wondered when the magic between Pauly and her had faded. Pauly cared more about the band than he did about her. Justine, Hazel thought, deserved a better shake.

Pauly leaned over the counter. "You don't sound too fired up."

"It's been a long day." Almost as an afterthought, Hazel added, "Makers Mark died."

"You mean the crazy old man you used to tell me about?" Pauly rarely hung out at Harley's.

"Yeah, that crazy old man." Hazel emptied the mesh fryer baskets into the garbage can.

"I'm sorry to hear that."

Hazel looked past Pauly at Justine who he wanted to say hello to. For a second he was encapsulated in the sounds of Harley's, the rumble of conversation, the squeak of barstools, the insistent bubbling of the fryer. *Fuck this noise*, Hazel thought.

Pauly was still leaning over the counter. He studied a girl's backside as she walked past him. "Yeah, so about this gig…"

***

They left for Bozeman on Friday afternoon. Hazel rode with Pauly and Justine in her GTO. Doug and Jason, with the drums and bass, followed in the station wagon. Justine drove. Hazel sat crammed in the back with the equipment, a mic stand digging into his side. Pauly and Justine argued briefly about what to listen to. Justine won out and they listened to The Talking Heads' *Fear of Music*. Hazel remained quiet and stared out the window, eying the grassy slopes and narrow ravines through which Blackfeet braves used to herd stolen horses.

Pauly turned down the stereo and looked back at Hazel. "Man, what's with you? Is it that regular from Harley's? You still bummed out about that old man?"

Hazel, his gaze snagged by clusters of trees and dilapidated barns, nodded. Pauly would not have made an effort to get to know Makers. Hazel watched the river bottom snake through alfalfa fields and cottonwood groves, every so often cutting beneath the freeway. He spoke slowly, with a wistful smile and a doleful light in his eyes. "Makers once told me about this woman he met in the bar and took upstairs to his place. They were getting acquainted on his mattress on the floor and she looked over and saw this blow-up doll and asked, 'What the hell is that?'" Here Hazel's composure was severed by an uncontainable laugh, but he quickly regained it. "And Makers said to her, 'Oh that, that's my old lady. But don't worry, she won't mind.'"

Pauly let out a laugh. Hazel saw Justine roll her eyes in the rear-view mirror. The river, which a moment before had been west of them, was now to the east. Hazel hadn't seen it meander under the freeway.

***

They pulled up in front of Farrah's house. Pauly and Justine got out and went inside. Hazel remained cramped in the backseat working up courage. The last time he'd seen Farrah he had been blacked out and far from smooth. This reintroduction would be awkward.

Once inside he was met by a wide-armed, pie-eyed, Farrah. "Drinky drink?" she asked.

He relaxed glad the party was already under way. "I've got the fixings for a vodka lemonade." He patted the brown paper bag under his arm.

"We've got cups in here."

Farrah led him through the living room. Another band on the night's bill was staying there also. The band members were camped on the floor, clustered around a large bulbous bong. Pauly and Justine had already joined the proceedings. Occasionally a leather jacket topped with long greasy hair would erupt in tremors of coughing. Hazel followed Farrah into the kitchen and saw half-empty bottles scattered across the kitchen counter. Hazel found a semi-clean cup, poured some McCormick Vodka, added some Country Time, some ice, and settled back against the counter. The sun shone through the window, illuminating the worn linoleum floor. Farrah leaned against the counter opposite him, sliding a little as she did so.

***

The Erratics' gig was a disaster. Hazel broke a string on the second song and attempted to borrow a guitar from the Japanese band that was headlining. After much haranguing, during which the guitarist thought Hazel was trying to steal his guitar and threatened to run him through with a cymbal stand, Hazel finally managed to borrow the guitar only to find it was in a different tuning. By the time they got things straightened out, it was time for the next band.

Adding to Hazel's misfortune was the arrival of Farrah's boyfriend, a listless slack-jaw with a ring in his nose and studs in his leather jacket, who didn't know Motörhead from the Misfits. The two of them spent the entire gig necking in front of the stage. Afterwards Hazel sat at the bar drinking whiskey with a vengeance trying to discern just what the hell it was the Japanese band was singing— some concoction of Englishnese with key phrases like "makin'fast machine," and "we go to rockin' tonight."

After the show a swaying Farrah made her way over to Hazel. He was surprised she was still in the picture. She leaned towards him, eyes peering from beneath drooping lids, lips searching for an elusive straw. "Hey, you wanna go steal some ether?"

"Ah, I think I'll pass on that one. It sounds like a good way to get arrested."

"Ah c'mon, it's really easy. It's in the labs on campus. All the lights are out. All we gotta do is go through the windows. Everybody's going."

Hazel couldn't think of anything more stupid to get arrested for. He shook his head.

"Charlotte's going," she added, her tone suggestive. She pointed to a girl, all curves and curls with fishnet stockings, who he had seen earlier. Again he shook his head. The girl came over to them. "Hey, you're in The Ecstatics. Awsome set," she said.

***

The lab was pitch-black. The sting of ammonia made his eyes water. Hazel could make out people silhouetted by the moon as they clambered through the window. Charlotte was ahead of him, crawling along on her hands and knees, giggling until she collided with a solid object, her frivolous laughter giving way to a drawn-out moan.

"Don't ignite the fumes!" someone whispered. "Keep the flames away."

He heard wallet chains and jewelry clinking in the darkness. Pauly and Justine were up on the counter in the corner, arguing in hissed whispers. Nearby a skeleton dangled on wheels, its white ribs luminous rungs. He heard excited whispers and Farrah's boyfriend exclaim, "Here it is!"

Hazel stopped crawling and got to his feet. Although he didn't know the way back to Farrah's, he knew he should bail. He was readying himself for a long walk when Justine emerged out of the black.

"Pauly is such an asshole. Oh my god, I can't believe him!" She whispered.

"Man, am I glad to see you," he said. "Let's get out of here."

"All right, but help me find my earring. I just dropped it on the counter."

He lit his Bic. The lighter's jiggling flame illuminated a row of jars and beakers. Hazel looked closer and froze.

It took him a minute to comprehend what he was seeing.

Resting in a jar of alcohol sat a brain. In looked like an outcropping of coral from the pages of *National Geographic*. There was a label across the jar. The lighter died and Hazel re-sparked it, burning his thumb. He shook his head, blinking, in order to be sure he had read it right. **M. Mulrooney, Missoula.**

***

When the others began opening the jars of ether, Hazel and Justine hurried to the window. Justine went first, and Hazel lowered the jar to her. As he dropped to the ground they heard laughter and wheels being rolled across the floor, probably the skeleton. He tensed at the sound of breaking glass. He doubted any of the others would make it out before the cops arrived. Justine handed him the jar. They could see the GTO parked beneath a tree. Never before had Hazel been so glad to see its primer-gray hulk. They spoke in tones both hushed and hurried as they made their way across the empty parking lot, its ordered symmetry lit by a row of street lights. Hazel had the brain tucked under his jacket.

"Holy shit. This is *Makers' brain*. Fucking *Makers Mark*. The Harley's regular. The dude who used to roadie for The Eagles."

Once in the car Justine said, "So it's some crazy old man's brain? What's the big deal? He was a big drinker and a ladies' man. You trying to learn something here? A new dog trying to learn old tricks? I'm not sure that thing's gonna be much help, but I'm sure the ladies will love it. I can just see you and some girl getting close, the lights are dimmed, and then she spies this pickled thinker and thinks you're Dr. Frankenstein." She pronounced it like Gene Wilder in *Young Frankenstein*. Hazel liked that.

"Listen, it's just for posterity's sake, and besides, if I could have any brain in my possession this would be the one. Except my own of course."

As they pulled out of the parking lot, Hazel held the jar gingerly in his lap. He pictured a ruffled Makers, coughing behind a clenched fist, the other hand extended in a subduing motion, *Whoa there, kid*, Makers would say, attempting a smile. *Take it easy.* Hazel looked in the direction of the lab as they started down the street. "What about Pauly?"

"Don't worry about it," she said, annoyed. "He can get a ride back with Jason and Doug in the morning."

***

Once on the freeway Justine put on *The Decline & Fall of the Upper Crust.* Hazel looked at her legs, her foot pressed against the accelerator, her neck bathed in the glow from the dashboard. It was strange, he thought, how normal it felt to be seated beside Pauly's girlfriend with Madrone "Makers Mark" Mulrooney's brain in a jar clenched between his thighs, just the three of them hurtling through the Montana night. It felt as if this is what they'd had planned all along. He thought how everything fabricated by man, the GTO, the stereo, his guitar, were all the result of brains. And those ethereal, unseen, unspoken thoughts. How could it be that they all came from the *same* place? Justine gave his thigh a squeeze and he felt a flicker of passion tear through him. Was this the work of brains too? He wanted to talk about this with her. He wanted to say something profound.

"I haven't had this much fun since I went A.W.O.L. in Managua," Hazel said.

"What was that?" She looked over at him.

His eyes traced the rims of buttes racing by, stars disappearing and re-emerging behind their flat crowns. Like those Blackfeet braves, he and Justine and Makers were making their own get-away. He looked down at the brain in his lap floating freely with the undulations of the road. He thought of all the bars it must have known, all the women it must have wooed. It was a goddamn good brain, he surmised. The night's frustrations and finds catching up with him, he began to drift off. Justine put on *Van Halen II*.

They reached Missoula just as the sun was coming up, the salmon sky reflected in the city's windows. As they exited the freeway, "Light up the Sky" came on. Hazel looked at Justine. She was all poise and purpose, yet relaxed and smiling. Listening to the music and looking at her, he thought, if ever there were a time *not* to think, to just *feel*, this might be it.

As they turned onto Broadway, Justine asked, "Is it alright if I crash at your pad? I'm wiped out."

When they got to his apartment, Hazel cleared a space on the table for the brain. He set it down carefully, a sacred chalice. The morning light filtered through the gilded liquid in which it floated like an embryo in a womb. He spun the jar slowly, following the fissures and grooves, struck by the mere fleshiness of it, the brain stem like the keel of a ship. Looking at it he felt vulnerable, distinctly aware of his own mortality. He thought of all it had known and seen. Had it ever been undone by despair? Had it known patience and reasoning—traits not recognizable in Makers? Was there a clue here to Makers Hazel could not see? When he held it he was sure it was resonating thoughtfulness, like the embers of a fire that's burned through the night. He could feel it through the glass. He got a drink of water before heading to bed. He pulled back the cover and slid in beside Justine.

"That was an unusual night," she said, turning toward him, her eyes closed.

He lay on his back and exhaled slowly. "It's pretty crazy shit. It makes you think."

"Uh-huh," she said, resting her chin on his shoulder.

"Makes you think too damn much is what it does."

She opened her eyes and took one last look around the room. She pointed at a teetering stack of milk crates filled with books. "I like that about you. You like them books."

He loved that she said it this way, *them books*. He was glad, that as a result of the night's course, he had not wound up here with Farrah or Charlotte beside him.

"I take it Maker wasn't much of a reader," she said, her eyes now closed again.

"Not to my knowledge. He was more about catching a buzz and chasing the ladies." He wondered about the things in a man's brain that might make him that way.

"And the occasional blow up doll."

"And the occasional blow up doll."

***

That night everyone congregated in Hazel's apartment, their recollection of the previous night in Bozeman fuzzy, fragmented. Pauly was the first to arrive, hung over, the taste of ether still in his mouth. He was wearing the same Iron Maiden shirt he had been wearing for a week. He did not ask about Hazel and Justine's return to Missoula. They did not volunteer any information.

"Go ahead, grab yourself a beer," Hazel told Pauly.

"You bet. I could use one." Pauly grabbed a beer and sat on the van seat. His eyes narrowed and he leaned toward the jar. "That's a brain!"

Hazel stood at the turn-table palming a record. He placed it on the spindle. "Take a look at whose brain it is," he said, gently lowering the needle.

Pauly eased the jar around and read aloud, "M. Mulrooney, Missoula." He looked up. "You've got to be kidding me. Is this for real?" He peered into the jar. "It looks real." He sat back and in a hushed tone of uncertainty remarked, "It's Makers Mark's mind? I don't fucking believe it." He then drew quiet.

Hazel recognized Pauly's silence. The brain had quieted him too, the realization that his own thoughts came from the firing of little electrons in a similar, spongy lump. The brain sat there like a jellyfish.

The rest of the gang arrived at odd intervals. Jason and Doug, who arrived after listening to a tape of the previous night's gig, were so dismayed by what they'd heard they failed to see the brain until after they were both on their second beer.

"What the hell is that?" Doug asked loudly, bent over the trunk.

"Is that what I think it is?" Jason said peering over Doug's shoulder.

When their friend Shawna arrived, Doug and Jason were so excited they almost gave it away. Hazel had put the jar in the fridge, fearful someone might knock it over. Now he was worried Makers might be getting cold. Shawna opened the fridge to get a beer. "Is that kimchee?" she asked casually.

"Actually," Jason said from the van seat, "that's Makers' brain."

Her face stamped with perplexity Shawna slowly pulled out a beer."Grody storm," she said and gently shut the door.

Hazel, hoping to infuse the energy in the room with some contemplation, put on Vangelis. He did not like them leaping around, hooting as if the brain were heisted loot. Makers deserved better.

They got it out of the fridge again.

"What if it warms up?" Jason said, "Senses our excitement? It might get some notions of its own and start swimming around."

"It is currently showing no signs of distress. Imagine if it started pulsing."

Doug set the jar on the trunk. Everyone crowded around except for Hazel. The banter, beer-fueled and boisterous, depressed him.

"Did you hear that Einstein's brain was bigger than normal?"

"Do you think it's a left-sided brain or a right-sided brain?"

"Considering what I've heard about Makers, I'm guessing it was some pretty scrambled action."

"Wonder what it would be thinking if it could still think?"

"It would probably be wondering where it could score."

"Or in pursuit of poontang."

"That's what I meant, Einstein."

Hazel let them talk and while they did he wondered if Makers might have had any children. Hazel had never heard him mention any, but figured, considering Makers' penchant for philandering, the chances were good, and if he did, what might they might think of the fact that their father's brain, having been stolen from a research lab was now the center piece for a rock n' roll party in Missoula, Montana.

***

Pauly and Justine went to get more beer. On their way out Hazel stopped them. "Don't go telling anyone about this. We gotta keep this under wraps."

"What do you say we take Makers down to Harley's?" Pauly suggested, his eyes half closed. "Buy him a drink?"

"Bad idea," Hazel said and shut the door behind them. He was okay with Justine and Pauly going to the store together. Justine's and his escape with the brain, the drive back to Missoula, and the morning spent together made him hopeful.

Hazel went to the record player and as he brought the needle out over a record he was lost in the spinning grooves, the record's surface suddenly too black for him to comprehend. There seemed to be an infinite number of grooves racing around and around, but he knew that was not the case and that the record would end. He wondered if that was how the brain worked, with a needle attached to the inside of the skull, slowly tracing all those grooves, mapping the mind and sparking thoughts in the process.

Hazel, still standing, took a long look around the room trying to... *fathom*—that was the word for it—how all the empty beer cans and scattered album covers, how the posters on his walls and books in the milk crates, how the music in his head and the conversation he chose to ignore, were all the result of cantaloupe-sized brains, squishy and gray, attached to brainstems. They were responsible for everyone's perception and understanding. And no one really cared.

***

Before the party was over he made his decision. When the morning came he would carry the brain over the bridge to where his truck was parked and drive it back to Bozeman. He hoped his truck would make it. It was not a fear of getting busted so much as it was a newfound respect for his own fragile mind. As the early morning hours passed by, he was overcome by this one penetrating thought, what would happen to all his hopes and dreams if and when *his* brain wound up in a jar?

When the sun came up, only Shawna remained, passed out on the van seat, the dregs of her Rainier slowly spilling on the floor. Hazel threw a flannel shirt over the jar and went out the door. Making his way down the stairs he thought of Madrone "Makers Mark" Mulrooney. He remembered the hat with the feathers and the loud, ratcheted laugh. *How ya doing, kid?* He remembered the women who had lined up to dance with Makers on his birthday, reminding him politely not to get fresh with them. "Alright," he'd bellow, "you'll just have to get fresh with me!" They had danced with him because despite the years of booze and wandering, there was real seduction in that crazy bastard. If there were one word to describe Makers, Hazel thought, what might it be? *Real? Unabashed? Carefree? Desirous?*

Hazel looked down at the jar in his hands. All that, he thought, reduced to just this. All that vigor, all that lust for life now floating unawares in a jug of alcohol, an ironically fitting end for the mind of Makers Mark Mulrooney.

Outside on the street Hazel blinked until his eyes adjusted to the light. He carried the jar awkwardly beneath the flannel, cradling it with both hands. Before crossing the Higgins Street Bridge, he stopped at a newspaper machine to adjust the jar and read the day's headline. As he did so, his eyes drifted to a heading listing local stories beneath which he read: **Laboratory break-in at Bozeman State, see page 8.**

Hazel straightened up and looked around self-consciously. He turned toward the bridge, walking quickly. There was little traffic. The only sound was the river's soft rumble as it passed below him. The sun, now fully up, filled the valley with a crisp light putting a pristine surface on the contours of the world.

Halfway across the bridge, the jar slipped from his fingers and shattered on the sidewalk, the sound of its breaking both a resounding clap and muffled crunch. Hazel bent down, his heart pounding, feeling regret crystalize inside him. He hesitated for a moment before removing the flannel shirt to reveal the brain resting in a pile of broken glass and a dark, oblong stain where the alcohol was already seeping into the pavement. The glass shards glinted in the morning sun. The brain, he noticed, was slightly flatter than it had been in the jar. Its slimy-wet surfaces and the broken glass painfully clear testimony to all that was temporary, to the ultimate disconnect. He examined the sky, searching for explanation in an untraceable blue. He saw the enormous white clouds wafting steadily westward, bulbous with folds like those of the brain.

Carefully he put his hand down beside the brain and with one slow, steady scoop, pushed it toward the lip of the bridge. When it reached the edge it dripped over the side before falling head-long, breaking apart a little in the air, shards of glass shimmering around it as they fell. The river roared, the glass sparkled, and that great, pickled, horny brain dropped like a stone. It hit the water with a soft plop that Hazel strained his ears to hear and then it was gone, swept away with the current. He pictured it tumbling slow-ly end over end, pushed by the green water, over smooth rocks, beneath downed logs, coming to rest in eddies and pools, before being carried onward. All that had been Madrone "Makers Mark" Mulrooney was now floating down the Clark Fork of the Blackfoot River, forever A.W.O.L. in the tributaries of Western Montana.

Hazel straightened up. Well, maybe Makers would have wanted it that way, he told himself. At least he's moving, going with the flow, until some big fish comes along and gobbles him up. He remem-bered that today they were having the wake at Harley's.

He turned and made his way back in the direction from which he'd come. The sun was in his eyes now. There was hardly any traffic, and the sound of the river was deep inside him, a soft vibration in the center of his mind. Here was a noise he could get behind. He reminded himself to wash his hands before breakfast.

SKYLER MCCURINE
Black. Woman.

I was always the only nigga in a room filled with white kids.
I see not much has changed.
I have known I was a Black child as early as four years old.

Looking around my hard-earned private school classroom, I felt
my difference, that something was askew like a wooden table with
a short leg. I was just, somehow....off. Even as a baby I knew that
my value was not that of my classmates. The words *I'm not right*
beat steadily alongside my heart. "I'm not right, I'm not right, I'm
not right."

Before you get your white guilt and assumptions all in a twist
and automatically ascribe the story line of Precious onto me—my
upbringing resembled that of the Huxtable kids (prior to Cosby's
allegations, it happened America, accept it).

I dressed like Denise, read like Sandra, was a sweet talking baby
like Rudy, and fuck what was Vanessa's purpose? She seriously
was the Blackest of Black sheep.

My father was a Rhodes Scholar, which is an international post-
graduate award for non-British students to study at the University of Oxford. As elaborated on in his will, Cecil Rhodes' goals in
creating the Rhodes Scholarships were to promote civic-minded
leadership among "young colonists" with "moral force of character
and instincts to lead," for the "recovery of the United States and
for the making the Anglo-Saxon race but one Empire."

My father, *Billy*, an inner city Chicago kid received this scholar-
ship enabling *William* to be the first Black partner in San Diego
County, and then a federal judge. In his courtroom, a defendant
named James Brown came to defend his case, my father looked at

him and said "James Brown huh, well, where's your new bag." The courtroom burst into laughter; Billy's humor has always helped William put others at ease. He also wears dope ass mutherfucking bowties, his interpretation of Cliff Huxtable's sweater.

My mother, Dana, is a real Claire-level Queen—an artist, every meal, wall, outfit is pure unfiltered expression. I remember her picking me up from school wearing a floor-length bejeweled Kafkan and limited edition Karl Lagerfeld shades, blasting "Bennie and the Jets" in our teal Saab. All I wanted was for her to wear Holiday-themed sweaters and light-up pins like my teachers and the other moms. I credit her stunning example and powerful aesthetic for my boogie-fancy-bitch ass that likes nice shit. Sue me. My mother is also tough, her love is often given in the form of brutal honesty, logic, and no frills delivery, and can be as curt and sharp as Claire's notorious side eye, which believe it or not was not the easiest for a cripplingly sensitive, skin-tuned outside elderly woman in child's body-person, like me.

I knew not to be arrogant about my Huxtable-like privilege, because I always felt like guests in these worlds and while I was wrapped in silk, I was made equally aware of my relationship with cotton.

Our jobs as tokens are to serve as an ambassador of our race, knowing that many will hang attributes to black skin after interacting with one of us. Our job is to carry Blackness with dignity, intelligence, and grace, as our grandparents and parents have. We do not speak for ourselves, we speak, behave, and carry ourselves with a dignity that honors the innocent blood of those who came before us, fought for my opportunity to not just stand in this room, but stand at the front of this room. We must represent our people well. Always. There will be many a time when you may want to cry, or laugh louder, or times in which your body is filled with so much rage but even when every part of you is screaming, you smile, say thank you and sometimes even, "Why yes, I can certainly handle more."

My parents exposed us to everything: museums, ballets, opera, swimming pools, piano camp: and there I would be: two afro puffs in a room filled with high pony tails and THOSE ONES COULD GET WET. My mother and father prayed every day for "a chocolate brown baby girl who would love the ocean, and play the piano better than Vladimir Horowitz." They very much wanted a dark brown baby girl, in some parts of the world the most unwanted thing. They were going to raise her to love herself even if that sent me kicking and screaming. Of which I am skilled. Our arguments over my hair being the worst. I had fucking wool instead of long flowing hair. Every time we went to the Beauty Supply store, to re-up on my natural hair care products, I whined over the Just For Me Box, a relaxer designed for young girls. I thought, "if only I too could have a side pony tail, Surely Zack Morris would fall in love with me then." My mother fought me daily, a battle of which I am grateful for. She fought to keep me black, she made me grapple with myself until I saw my features for what they are, beautiful. I learned to not shy away from environments in which I was different and come my sophomore year of high school, she found another opportunity for me to harness my TOKEN power. She became drawn to the whitest sport in the world, threading our love of water within it: rowing. My mother signed us up for a free class at the Mission Bay Aquatic Center; a week later I joined San Diego Rowing Club's Junior team. My novice year wasn't too bad; I had the old pains of "I'm not right, I'm not right" but made a few solid friends, lost some LBs and was even being eyed for the Varsity team.

Novice year, while intimidating, felt like Kindergarten: safe, complimentary, and fun, but my Varsity year resembled Middle School. All of these teenagers, and unlike Novice year, there were actual boys here. WTF. I went to an all-girls school and my friends and I had real contests to see who could grow their leg hair the longest in the winter. I did not DO teenage boys: in both ways. I have always hated spending time socializing with my peer group when guys were present. The girls became catty and the boy's imbeciles. I have always been a 60 year old woman—chain smoking in a chaise lounge, preferring to hang out with the parents vs. my peers.

So there I was, a 60 year old colored girl, who was now Team Captain of the Varsity team. Unlike other sports, crew is all year long, August through May, practice is 6 days a week, sometimes 4 A.M. practice before school and 4 P.M. after school. We had regattas, or races, at least once a month, sometimes twice. Regattas take over the whole weekend: wake up at two, get to Long Beach by four, prepare the boats, assemble the tracks, unload the giant truck, race all day, sometimes four races, 1.5 miles each each, sometimes 3.7 miles, then break down each boat. The best parts about racing was I knew my parents would take me to In-N-Out after. I was racing harder not to improve my time but to the tray of animal fries that were waiting for me once I finished.

I loved late night rows, chasing the rare moment when the boat is perfectly balanced and the oars don't touch the water until all eight people drop them in together and pull with raw power. My most favorite memories are of late night rows during red tide, which came frequently during late spring. Every time our oars touched plopped into the bay, Hpnotiq liqueur colored water would trail behind us. These bliss filled moments accounted for 10% of my experience rowing; the other 90% was a test in surviving the social realms.

The JV and Varsity teams were comprised of kids who had a second chance at popularity; in their respective high schools they were somewhere in the middle, but at crew they had the chance to be the belles of the ball, the hot guy, so their propensity for cruelty was even stronger because they had something to prove, mostly to themselves. Issues on land always translated to issues on water. The person responsible for buffing out our issues was Varsity coach, Greggory Trail Logut. He did not live up the name Trail. Trail insinuates adventure, color, nature... he was more like a barren dessert than a trail. Everyone has had a manager whose technical skills led them to a promotion but they are completely void of emotional intelligence and people skills. That was Greg, a great rower, technically skilled but not capable of leading. The last person who with whom one should entrust the self esteem of the most vulnerable demographic: teenage girls. He turned a blind eye to the fact that he had the rare opportunity to use his voice to protect, encourage, or improve the sheep under his watch. Even worse, he sometimes, however discreetly, participated in excluding the weaker, slower, dorkier kids on the team. Dorky kids like Sarah.

Her government name was Sarah, but she went by Haruka, after a Japanese anime character. She refused to shave her legs, had a bowl haircut, and to make matters worse she looked exactly like the stereotypical character of a harsh German masseuse. There's always that one kid that just can't process anger, they heave when they're frustrated, having a literal tantrum; that was Haruka. She had weekly explosions, and truthfully, many of them were warranted: she expressed her frustration at people's shiftiness and bullying while the rest of us hid it. When red-faced Haruka cried and stormed off, everyone either laughed or rolled their eyes. Greg, frustrated by a need to use empathy, compassion, or kindness, would send me after her, you know, to do his fucking job of coaching.

Come my second year on Varsity, a kid standing at 6'7" joined the team. Ryan Stewt wore black eyeliner, a spiked collar, his box-dyed jet black hair resembled a bob—it was rumored last year, his novice year, that he was a Nazi and proud racist. Every time I walked by him I felt a chill. His darkness terrified me, and I made sure to always contort myself around him: to walk around him vs. next to him.

It was fall: we were a few months into the season, we had just carried the boats in and were washing them down, only 30 more minutes until I can go home, only seven more months until I'm done, I thought.

Ryan was picking on a little novice kid, a freshman who was a coxswain, coming in around 90 pounds. He was dangling his shoe in the air, laughing, and watching his little minion struggle. The blonde curly-haired kid laughed, trying to pass it off that he was in on the joke but we all knew better. The next 30 seconds are a blur;

my boat mates swirled around me, pushing me forward, encouraging me to defend this kid. "You're the team captain, Sky, make him stop." Go. Before I could formulate an answer I was standing before him. I had to force each word out, my voice cracked, "Return his shoe. Now." He paused, looking at me coolly. "What the fuck did you say?" FUCK. FUCK. I try harder, firmer, standing taller. "I said, give him his shoe now." "What the fuck is it to you, bitch?" My boat mates ushered me away telling him off, "Smart move jackass, telling off the team captain." I went home, trembling. He would have hit me, possibly worse if this had been the 50s, 60s, 70s, fuck it, if there were fewer people around, if it would have just been us. He would have hit me, possibly worse. I went home and did what every respectable teenager in 2003 did: I logged onto my AOL account, screename Afros4eo4, and Moti, my long time sister and only other Black chick on the team, forwarded Ryan's away message. She warns me, preps me to stay calm, as allies do: I open it.

"This bitch tried to step to me today. I will fucking kill her. I hate Black people"

I didn't feel comfortable being at practice and was forced to tell my parents about what had happened. They made me tell Greg, and Ryan was suspended for a few days. My dad and I had to have a meeting with Greg the next day; Ryan and his dad were to follow. My father and I sat down and had a real conversation in which he shared his horrific experience of being chased by an angry mob for going to the beach with my grandma. He reminded me that "it is my duty to serve as an extension of Christ" he said, "To forgive, to love." Greg told me it's my choice, to kick Ryan off of the team or let him stay. I was doing his job again.

There was no space for me to react the way I felt called to: I must take on the burden of my people before me: lift my head, show up the next day, and extend undeserved grace. People sang hymns of joy during beatings because it's the boldest act of defiance. You can take my body but you can't take my joy. So I sang the hymn, as loudly as I could: I let Ryan stay on the team. My father followed with, "Ryan stays, on one condition, he is to be treated as an equal, the same as everyone else. He is not to be an outcast." Greg nodded his head. Ryan came back to practice, Greg sent the the men's and women's teams on a five mile run, and Ryan breezed past me. My run turned into a jog and then a walk, the weight of my blackness was too heavy. Greg said nothing to me about what had transpired. My teammates had moved on, the novelty of gossip had worn off. I'm not a rower anymore. I don't want to be.

My parents being the steadfast, loyal and solid-as-oak puritan Christians that they are, had a firm stance on suffering--it does a body good. If Jesus could do it, through his grace, you can too. My parents placed me on the proverbial platform of the ambassador's perseverance and forced me to honor my commitment to the team. So, I fought back. I didn't speak to them. One day, then five, then seven, not. one. word. My silence was loud and clear: My parents finally let me quit.

My silence towards my parents was the first time I really mustered womanly courage. I stood up for myself, boasting the audacious truth that I knew what was best for me, better than my peers, coach, or parents.

The first time I sang a hymn in the face of ugly.
The first I had the audacity to buy into my body, my choice.
The first time I placed myself above the duty of ambassadorship.
The first time I said THIS ISN'T RIGHT vs. I'm not right.
I earned the first of many threads that would make up the intricate and ornate weaving of a Black woman.

CONTRIBUTORS

CL BLEDSOE is the assistant editor for *The Dead Mule* and author of sixteen books, most recently the poetry collection *Trashcans in Love* and the flash fiction collection *Ray's Sea World*. He lives in northern Virginia with his daughter.

ALEX BOSWORTH was born in a house he built himself in San Diego circa 1965. His parents were both teachers with theatrical backgrounds who encouraged him to write and read his stories before unwilling audiences from the age of ten. Alex's collection of short stories, *Chip Chip Chaw: Tales of the Unsane* is available online.

MARISA CRANE is a web content editor in San Diego. She is the author of one full-length book of poetry and three chapbooks and her poetry has appeared in *Apeiron Review*, *Glassbook Magazine*, *Spark: A Creative Anthology*, and *Circus Magazine*.

LINDA M. CRATE is a Pennsylvanian native born in Pittsburgh yet raised in the rural town of Conneautville. Her poetry, short stories, articles, and reviews have been published in a myriad of magazines both online and in print. She has three published chapbooks *A Mermaid Crashing Into Dawn* (Fowlpox Press - June 2013), *Less Than A Man* (The Camel Saloon - January 2014), and *If Tomorrow Never Comes* (Scars Publications, August 2016). Her fantasy novel *Blood & Magic* was published in March 2015. The second novel of this series *Dragons & Magic* was published in October 2015. The third of the seven book series *Centaurs & Magic* was published November 2016. Her novel *Corvids & Magic* was published March 2017.

CAT DIXON is the author of *Eva* and *Too Heavy to Carry* (Stephen F. Austin University Press, 2016, 2014) and *The Book of Levinson* and *Our End Has Brought the Spring* (Finishing Line

Press, 2017, 2015). She is the managing editor of The Backwaters Press. Her poetry and reviews have appeared in numerous journals including *Sugar House Review*, *Midwest Quarterly Review*, *Coe Review*, *Eclectica*, and *Mid-American Review*.

CRAIG EVENSON is a school teacher. He shares a house with a number of creatures, including a woman. He lives in Northfield, Minnesota.

ELAINE GINGERY has a degree in Creative Writing though has spent the last 20 years working primarily in the performing arts. Currently she works as a bookkeeper for her family business, at a grocery store, and writes when she can catch a free hour. Her work has been featured in So Say We All's VAMP program as well as in The Hausmann Quartet / SSWA Collaboration, "The 7 Last Words of Christ." This is her first piece to be featured in a written collection. She spends her free time working on her small urban farm, tending goats, chickens, a rapidly expanding orchard, and snacking off the lush garden. She has a couple of kids, one husband, and a home designed by a famous architect. It leaks. Obviously.

GERARDO DE JESUS GURROLA JR. is a writer, wrong-er, lover, fighter, lover, and he writes more at entrentre.wordpress.com.

LAURA GWYNNE has been drawing around since '84.

DAVID HENSON is pursuing a PhD in English at the University of Nebraska-Lincoln. His work has appeared at *Fluland*, *Big Bridge*, and won the 2016 Problem House Press short story contest . He writes and records music under the name Shadows on a River, which can be heard at shadowsonariver.bandcamp.com. He tweets @davidbhenson.

NOLAN HUTTON is a special education teacher in San Marcos, CA where he lives gratefully with his wife and son. He studied creative writing and literature at San Francisco State University. His prose and poetry can also be found in *The Acorn Review*, *Monkeybicycle*, *deLuge Journal* and *Whiskey Island Magazine*.

PHILIP KUAN is an aspiring Californian writer with a passion for befuddling readers. Some of his favorite authors include Charles Dickens, Tolkien, and Franz Kafka, among others. He has been published in several short story magazines, and is always looking for constructive feedback at philkuan.wordpress.com.

KATHLEEN LANGSTROTH feels compelled to glue words together. She has only recently started sending out my work. Until now, she was unpublished as a short story writer. She loves the short story with all its inherent challenges. She will continue to do battle with this format into the foreseeable future. She remains convinced that it is the perfect platform to reach out to a world of readers. She hopes everyone can absorb something they find meaningful to take away with them.

YVONNE HIGGINS LEACH is the author of *Another Autumn* (WordTech Editions, 2014). Her poems have appeared in many journals and anthologies. A native of Washington state, she earned a Master of Fine Arts from Eastern Washington University. She spent decades balancing a career in communications and public relations, raising a family, and pursuing her love of writing poetry. Now a full-time poet, she splits her time living on Vashon Island and in Spokane, Washington. For more information, visit www.yvonnehigginsleach.com.

TONI MARTIN is a physician and writer, currently a regional medical consultant for the disability program of Social Security. In addition to practicing medicine, she published two books of non-fiction. The second, *When the Personal Was Political: Five Women Doctors Look Back*, appeared in 2008. Over the last ten years, her stories and essays have appeared in *The East Bay Monthly*, *The Threepenny Review*, *The Los Angeles Review* and *The Bellevue Literary Review*. She and her husband live in Berkeley, CA. As a child, she visited her grandparents in Savannah, GA.

NICOLE MARTINEZ is a freelance copywriter and hobby blogger who currently resides in Central Wisconsin. You can find her online at lyrical.7and1.net, reviewsbycole.com, and 7and1.net or in person stalking the nearest cemetery. When not walking or writing, Nicole lives a nerd life full of video and board games, comic books, science, cats, and ridiculous wordplay. She's also a sex-positive feminist hellbent on fostering positive dialogues about sex. Send cat memes and dad jokes to @anaesthetic on Twitter.

KEVIN MCCOY lives and works in Colorado. His collection *Tea in a Bowl* was published by Unsolicited Press.

SKYLER MCCURINE is redefining the look of leadership as a personal stylist, public speaker, wonder woman through her business Le Red Balloon. Driven by the lackluster stereotypical portrayal of women in the media and the devastating landscape of leadership (male/pale/stale leadership) she leads workshops for teenage girls and professional women around leadership, parity, self acceptance, personal branding, and of course, style. Skyler's passion for fostering leadership, audacity, and courage in young women led her to an invitation to TEDx, to SD Business Journal's "Emerging Generation Award" and to her recent invitation to attend the Forbes Under 30 Summit as Swiss Luxury watch brand Baume & Mercier's guest of distinction. She was a finalist for the 2016 Forbes 30 Under 30 list in the social entrepreneurship category. She is a native San Diegan and received her BA in Communication Studies from Loyola Marymount University and MA in Organizational Management from Ashford University. Her fervent belief in inclusion, red balloons, and champagne are her personal North Stars.

PAUL DOUGLAS MCNEILL II is a writer and English professor living in the Arctic Circle of Alaska and teaching at a tribal college. His poems and short stories have appeared in *The Maynard, Quail Bell Magazine*, and *Off the Coast*.

BRETT MORRIS was born in Australia in 1958, moved to America in 1962, joined the Air Force in 1976, in and out of college since 1986, trained to work on museum exhibits and heavy trucks, lifelong frustrated writer.

LUCY PALMER is from England but now lives in beautiful San Diego with her small family. By day, she runs a copywriting business and by night, she can be found either hanging out with her aforementioned little family, playing her trumpet, or taking the odd creative writing class at the excellent Grossmont college. Lucy has had poetry published in a few journals and recently had a prose poem nominated for Best Small Fictions 2017. She's thrilled to have her first short story published by *The Radvocate*. She tweets @lucyprich.

POUYA RAZAVI is a father, husband, technologist, philosopher and writer. Born in Tehran, he is based in London, England.

STEVE TAGUE claims that the best way to find him is to not seek him out. He lives on the remote edges of society (some would say that is where its heart truly lies), sowing sordid tales of sex and succor. He will not be suffered by the vapid masses, but rather make them be suffered by him, preferring instead the company of harlots and hussies, lost lovers and jilted jerks, the dregs, droogs, slags, hags, dirtbags, junkies, flunkies, actors, detractors and of course your friendly neighborhood bartenders. He's been compared to such prolific writers as Hemingway ("That guy is definitely no Hemingway."), Dostoevsky ("Just a talentless thrift store Dostoevsky.") and Pynchon ("He's like Pynchon, but, you know... shitty."), and his mother will tell you he's "very talented, and good looking. He needs to work on his attitude though." Hard living is not for the weak. You don't seek the edge so you can see by what boundary you will be confined. You seek it so you can see what's on the other side. It takes a particular type of constitution to be able to plumb the darkest treads of our collective humanity, question what they mean and know when they've been truly lost. It is the duty of those who are able to explore these depths, then come back and report on it to those too afraid to take the trip. The weak will falter, perish or go mad. The hard will burn the world down...

AMANDA TUMMINARO lives in the US. Her poetry has appeared in *Cottonwood*, *Spoon River Poetry Review* and *Freshwater*, among others. She is also a big fan of music, some of her favorite artists being The Beatles, Madonna, Ray Charles, Johnny Cash and Patsy Cline. She is currently working on her first poetry chapbook.

JED WYMAN received his MFA in Creative Writing from Oregon State University in 2009, and he currently teaches writing at Southwestern Oregon Community College in Coos Bay. Prior to this he spent two summers teaching in Kenya, twelve summers building trails and packing mules in Sequoia National Park, and playing guitar in a number of craptastic rock bands including Grim Reefer (Bard College, New York) and Non Drowsy (Missoula, Montana). His stoies have appeared in *The Masthead*, *The Bangalore Review*, and *34thParallel*, and have been shortlisted for Writecorner Press's E.M. Koeppel Award. He is grateful for epiphanies.

DONNA ZEPHRINE was born in Harlem, New York and grew up in Bay Shore, Long Island. She went to Brentwood High School. She graduated from Columbia University School of Social Work in May 2017 and she presently works for the New York State Office of Mental Health at Pilgrim Psychiatric Center Outpatient SOCR (State Operated Community Residence). She is a combat veteran who did two tours in Iraq. She was on Active duty Army stationed at Hunter Army Airfield 3rd Infantry Division. Her job in the military was a mechanic. She has participated in various writing workshops such as the Veterans Writing Workshop at Fordham Lincoln Center, and has been recently published in an anthology entitled *Afterwords*. She was also published in New York University's Veteran's Writers Workshop's anthology *9 Lives*, *Bards Annual 2017*, *The Local Gem Press*, *War Writer's Campaign* and *Blogground*. She is also a contributing member to other writing workshops, the Voices From War and Project 9 Line workshop. Currently Donna is studying for her licensing in social work but tries to continue with her creative writing whenever she can. She also is involved in World Team Sports, Wounded Warrior Project and Team Red White and Blue. In her spare time she enjoys sled hockey, kayaking, cycling and is always willing to try new adventures.